Project Management

In easy steps is an imprint of In Easy Steps Limited
Southfield Road · Southam
Warwickshire CV47 0FB · United Kingdom
www.ineasysteps.com

Notice of Liability
Every effort has been made to ensure that this book contains accurate
and current information. However, In Easy Steps Limited and the
author shall not be liable for any loss or damage suffered by readers
as a result of any information contained herein.

Trademarks
All trademarks are acknowledged as belonging to their respective
companies.

Printed and bound in the United Kingdom

ISBN-13 978-1-84078-370-4
ISBN-10 1-84078-370-2

Contents

1 The Basics

This chapter defines what a project is, what we mean by project management and what it requires to manage a project.

Introduction

To be successful, project managers need to complete a project on time, within budget and with the needs of the business fully met. Whether your project is large or small, the methods and processes set out in this book will show you how to deliver the desired results every time.

The majority of projects that fail do so for one very simple reason, a lack of adequate project management. By understanding what's involved in managing a project and using the approach set out in this book you can ensure that your project will be successful.

Successful Project Management

Successful project management is not rocket science, it's just good, old fashioned, common sense together with some basic management skills.

There are four basic management skills that a project manager needs in order to be successful:

- Planning: a lack of adequate planning is the single most common cause of project failure, so this really is a key skill

- Organizing: making sure everything happens when it needs to and not too soon or too late

- Leading: the people working on the project and all the other project stakeholders

- Controlling: in order to measure and track progress, and report on it

Follow the steps set out in this book and you will develop these four key skills.

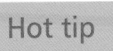

Hot tip

These are the four key skills that every project manager needs to develop.

What is a Project?

To start at the beginning, what do we mean by a project? Put simply it is a series of tasks or activities that have to be carried out in order to bring about a change or achieve some other identified objective. The project could be a personal one such as learning a foreign language, a construction project like building a house, or it could be to implement some new business venture.

Key Characteristics

Whatever type of project it is, there are three key characteristics that can be associated with it:

1 It must have a goal (some sort of specific outcome), as there would be no point in carrying out a project if it did not achieve anything of benefit

2 It must be started or initiated, as projects do not happen spontaneously

3 It needs someone (the project manager) to run it and steer it through to achievement of the goal

So a project is the implementation of a change, with a beginning, middle and an end. It will also have a time frame, it will be unique (every project is different in some way), people are involved and it will usually have finite resources (people, time and money).

Project Life Cycle

The beginning, middle and end stages of a project all have their own particular characteristics and their own requirements. This book covers the complete project life cycle, starting with the correct way begin a project (chapter 2), through however many middle stages there are (chapter 10), to the final stage of closing the project down and learning from it (chapter 11). This whole approach is based on common sense and best practice developed over many years and countless successful projects.

Don't forget

Every project is unique, don't assume it will work out exactly the same as the last one.

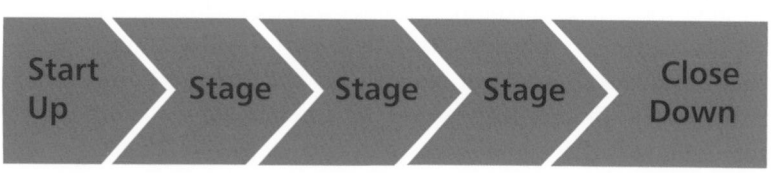

Start Up > Stage > Stage > Stage > Close Down

Project Management

So what sort of skills does a project manager need and can anyone do it? In practice project management requires many of the basic management skills that a line manager needs, but it also requires a different approach.

Hot tip

Project management requires common sense and a structured approach. This book will give you the structured approach.

Can Anyone Do It?

Project management does not require any magic gift, just some common sense coupled with a structured approach to things. Assuming that you, the reader, possess common sense (the purchase of this book would certainly suggest it!) this book will provide you with a structured approach to managing projects.

Line Management

Let's start by considering what's involved in traditional or line management. Typically this would involve managing a department or a group of people, so first of all you need people to manage. Then you would need objectives for what you have to achieve with the group of people. Then you would need some sort of budget (expenditure for the people and other resources you will use and revenue or targets for the output of the group). Having these things in place you can get on and manage the business process by allocating and scheduling people's work, developing and motivating the people, reviewing their performance and giving them feedback. It does not matter what the group is doing, the management process is the same. To differentiate this from project management it is referred to as process management.

Project Management

Now if we consider managing a project, are there any of the preceding things you won't need to have or do as a project manager? The only possible item is 'developing people' which is not usually a project management responsibility (although it could be if someone is permanently allocated to a project manager). The lists are very similar. To manage a project you will need agreed objectives. You will need people to work on the project. You will need a budget for the people and other resources you will use. You will also need targets for what you will produce.

You will need to allocate and schedule people's work and, while you might not be responsible for people's development, you will still need to motivate them. While you might not review their performance, you will still need to review their work and give them feedback.

So in summary there are not that many differences between the line or process management role and the project management role; and most of those differences are quite subtle. As a project manager you will still need the same sort of infrastructure. You will still have to do the same sort of management tasks and consequently you will need the same sort of skills. The real difference between the two roles is that line management is the management of an on-going process, while project management is the management of change.

Don't forget

Project management is the management of change.

Managing a Project

As we saw in the preceding topic, line management involves the management of a process. Your department, division or business will continue answering calls, sending out invoices or producing widgets as long as you stay in business. Project management on the other hand is the management of change.

Management of Change

You will be changing (perhaps radically) the way things are done which is very different from managing the doing of them. The project manager requires all the basic management skills together with the ability to manage change. So let us look at some of the project or change related activities that are involved in the role as these are the key things the project manager will need to do to stay in control.

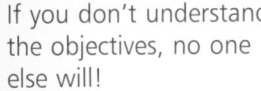

Beware

If you don't understand the objectives, no one else will!

Clarify the objectives

Projects often start out with poorly defined objectives (if any). You will need to resolve these and get them agreed with senior management before the project can properly start.

Develop the plan

Planning is probably the single most important activity a project manager has to carry out. But it's not a one-off activity, the project plan will need to be evolved and adapted through the life of the project.

Manage the risks

Change always involves risks and these risks are compounded by the uncertainty and unknown that will exist at the start of a project. It is therefore essential to carry out some sort of risk assessment exercise as early as possible in the project. Failure to do so could result in the project getting knocked off the rails by the first thing that goes wrong. Risk management is critical to the success of a project.

Manage and motivate the team

As project manager you do not usually have line management responsibility for the team, but you still have to keep the team managed and motivated. In fact, it is even more important if you don't have direct managerial authority for the people in the team.

Communicate with everyone

People need to know what's happening on a project. Not just the people on the project team but everyone who is affected by it.

Measure progress against plan

The project manager needs an accurate way of measuring project progress and, having measured it, they need to keep everyone in the picture about how the project is going.

Deal with problems

Problems will occur, so you need to plan for them and deal with them. If you have identified potential risks you can make contingency plans for them, but if you haven't you will need to deal with any problems before they cause a major upset.

Steer the project to a successful conclusion

As well as dealing with day to day issues the project manager has also to retain the big picture and make sure the project stays on track to its destination.

Hot tip

Communicate with everyone involved on or affected by your project.

13

4 Steps to Success

Earlier we defined a project as having a beginning, a middle and an end. We can build on that definition and expand it into four steps to a successful project.

1 Identify your objective or goal, what the project is trying to achieve, and agree it with all concerned

2 Plan how you are going to get there and decide how you are going to measure progress against the plan

3 Carry it out by managing the project until you have achieved your objectives

4 Hand it over; you have achieved your objectives and your job is done

Beware

Never ever be tempted to dive straight in at step two or three.

It sounds simple and it is, but it is amazing how many people just want to dive in at step three and get on with it. The other problem the same people have is with step four, letting go. If they haven't defined their objectives or planned the project properly, the chances are that it will never be quite right. They will keep having to make changes until they have finally understood the business objectives. This is what they should have done, but probably failed to do, in step one!

Responsibility & Authority

When you are asked to manage a project (or perhaps told to) you are effectively being asked to take responsibility for it. Accepting that responsibility is the commitment that you make to your organization.

Responsibility

Lack of accountability is a common reason for project failure. It is absolutely essential, if a project is to be successful, that the project manager accepts full responsibility for it. They are responsible if it goes well and they are equally responsible if it goes badly. They need to understand the objectives and be clear on why it matters to their organization.

Authority

The other side of the coin is that once the project manager has accepted responsibility for a project, then the organization must give them sufficient authority to carry it out. It is a basic tenet of management that you cannot have responsibility without being given an equal level of authority.

Delegation

The organization is delegating to the project manager. In the same way the project manager will be delegating responsibility and authority to the people working on the project.

Control

The final part of this process is control. When delegating tasks to team members you still have responsibility for ensuring they carry them out correctly. This means having some form of control. The more significant the task, or the more inexperienced the delegate, the more control you need to keep over it. But good delegation is about trusting people and allowing them to get on with it, while still being there to help if they need assistance.

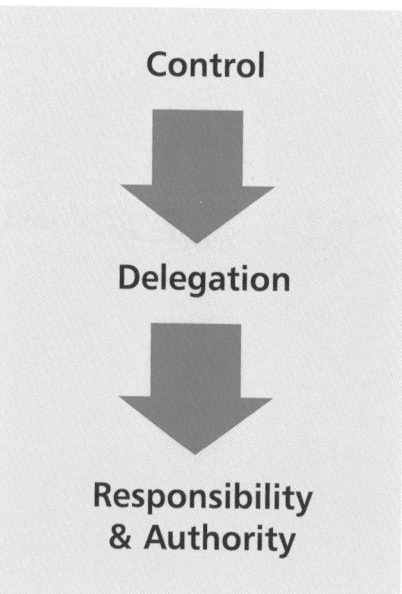

Control

↓

Delegation

↓

Responsibility & Authority

Beware

If you don't fully support a project, then don't accept it.

Hot tip

Trust your team and delegate to them but make sure you stay in control.

Good Project Managers

We all want to be seen as good project managers, but what exactly makes someone a good project manager?

Successful Project Management

Well for a start a good project manager will be a successful project manager. They will have a record of managing projects that have been successful. But there are other things we can also observe in successful project managers, so if you want to be a successful project manager follow these steps:

1. Be committed to the project, believe in it and actively support it

2. Be a good motivator and make everyone feel they really are part of the team

3. Delegate by using the skills and abilities of the team members and acknowledge their work

4. Know and understand what the business needs from the project and communicate it to the team

5. Believe in yourself and know where you are going, the team will be looking to you for a lead

6. Be seen to be making progress by keeping track of each piece of work that the team completes

7. Be well organized, nothing is more worrying than a disorganised project manager

8. Stay in control of things; if you don't know what's going on the project is likely to go off the rails

9. Be proactive rather than reactive and communicate with everyone involved with the project

Carry out these nine steps and you too will be a successful project manager.

Hot tip

Make sure you really understand the business needs.

Be Successful

As a project manager, if you do and are seen to do the things listed on the page opposite, you will be successful. That together with sound common sense, a basic management knowledge and a good understanding of your business will ensure you stay successful.

In the introduction to the book, we identified four key skills that every project manager needs to have. These were Planning, Organizing, Leading and Controlling. But there is one other key skill that a successful project manager needs to have:

Communications

Good project managers are also good communicators. You don't have to be an eloquent orator, you just need to be able to talk to people. Ask them how they are and how their work is going. Tell them what you are doing and why. And never forget that communication is a two way process. As well as talking to people, you also need to be able to listen to them and take in what they have to say.

We will be looking at communication under several topics later in the book but for now start by thinking about who you need to communicate with. It isn't just the project team although you certainly need to communicate with them.

Hot tip

Learn to communicate with people on a regular basis and you will be a better project manager.

Project Management Style

One thing anyone new to project management may need to do is adapt their style of management.

Negotiation

Although a project manager will have people on their project team, at best they will be seconded, but more likely they will be shared with their regular line managers. So instead of being able to tell people what to do, the project manager will have to negotiate with them (and probably their line managers as well) and agree what they will do and when they will do it. This requires negotiation and the ability to relate to and see things from other people's points of view.

Prioritization

Most small project teams have no or very few full-time project team members, so the part-time team members will have other work commitments and other priorities. The project manager must be able to discuss priorities and agree them with the team members (and again with their line managers). This can become a real problem, particularly if schedules need to be changed (and they probably will) during the course of the project. The project manager needs to be able to negotiate and renegotiate as necessary.

Communication

As the project manager you need to communicate with the project team, the project sponsor and the wider stakeholder group. You will need to communicate well and you will need to communicate often. It is not a one-off process, to ensure the success of the project you will need to keep on communicating.

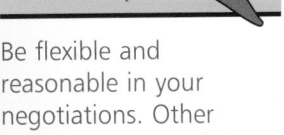

Hot tip

Be flexible and reasonable in your negotiations. Other people are more likely to be reasonable if you are.

Getting Commitment

It is essential that the project manager gains the team's full and complete 'buy in' to the aims and objectives of the project and their understanding of the priorities, as these may well be very different from the day to day priorities of the business. In short the project manager must 'sell' the project to the team members, their managers and everyone else in the business.

Delegation

If it's starting to sound as if the project manager needs to be some sort of 'Lone Ranger' complete with 'silver bullets' that's not the case. In fact, it is just the opposite. They will not be able to do everything themselves. If they try to, they will quickly alienate the team. So the project manager must delegate effectively.

Effective delegation is all about recognizing and using people's skills and getting the most suitable person to do each task. Again this needs to be negotiated and evaluated against all the other requirements, to get the best overall results for the project.

Documentation

All of the above discussions and agreements must be documented and copied to the team members (and their line managers where relevant) so that there is no room for misunderstanding. That is not to say the team members cannot be trusted but very few of us have a perfect memory. A brief list of tasks, to whom allocated and when they need to be done by, acts as an excellent reminder.

Leadership

Project managers need to be open, build trust with their teams and motivate them in order to build the team spirit necessary for a successful project team. What they have to demonstrate is real leadership. Not the sort that comes from being 'a star' but the sort that gets built by showing that they are ready to lead by example. To take decisions and accept responsibility for them, to admit mistakes and build on them, to encourage and build the team: that is real leadership.

Project managers are 'enablers' rather than 'doers', they must be able to help and facilitate other people's work. If they don't trust their team, their team won't trust them. They need to help others to do the right thing rather than doing it themselves. Then people will have pride in their work and will believe it really is a team.

Hot tip

Work on building team spirit by occasionally organizing a fun event. It's a great way to motivate people.

Summary

- A project is a series of tasks or activities that need to be carried out in order to bring about a change

- Every project must have a clearly stated goal or objective, it needs to be initiated and it needs someone (the project manager) to steer it to a successful conclusion

- Projects will take place within a time frame, every one is unique, it will involve people and it will usually have finite resources available

- Successful project management is about getting projects completed on time, within budget and with the business needs fully met

- To manage a project successfully you need basic common sense and a structured approach. You provide the common sense and this book will provide the structured approach

- Project managers need to manage change, clarify objectives, develop a plan, analyze risks, manage and motivate the team, measure progress and deal with problems in order to steer the project to a successful conclusion

- There are four steps to a successful project: identify the objective, plan how you will get there, carry it out and then hand it over as your job is done

- Make sure you take full responsibility for your project and make sure you get sufficient authority to be able to carry it out

- Project managers need to develop four key skills: Planning, Organizing, Leading and Controlling

- Effective delegation is about recognizing and using people's skills to carry out suitable tasks

- Good project managers are successful project managers and they never forget to communicate

- Project managers need to develop a style of management that uses negotiation, prioritization, selling the project, delegation, documentation and leadership

2 Getting Started

Starting up a project in the right way is critical to project success. This chapter will show you how to identify stakeholders, select the team, agree the terms of reference and then start the planning process.

Starting a Project

The aim of this chapter is to cover what could be the most crucial part of the project, starting it up and working out who should be on the project team. The reason it is critical is that you usually only get one chance to start a project, so you better make sure you start it right.

It's Exciting

Let us be honest, starting anything new is exciting, the rush of adrenalin and maybe a little bit of apprehension. You might be tempted to just get stuck straight in to your new project and get on with it. You might well be told to do so, the business wants results and it wants them now (if not sooner)! It should of course know better.

Controlled Start

This chapter sets out an approach to starting a project in a controlled way. Even if your project has already started, you can still use this chapter as a checklist and back-fill anything that might have been missed. The effort required at this stage will be more than rewarded in the later stages of the project.

Beware

If there is no clear business case and no business ownership, then stop the project.

Why It's Important

The reason it's important is that it represents the first opportunity the project manager will get to stop the project! That's right, if there is no clear business case or the business is not prepared to 'own' it, then it should never be allowed to see the light of day.

Where Projects Come From

Projects often begin in a fairly unstructured way. Someone in the organization gets a good idea for a new business venture and depending on how senior they are, they may get instant support or they may have to argue their case.

Project Start Up

Wherever the project has come from, the following are the main steps that should happen as a project starts up. Your project may already be part way through this process, but even so go back and check that these steps have been carried out.

1. Idea: All projects start with some sort of idea. Perhaps a better way of doing something, perhaps something new, perhaps a business relocation

2. Feasibility: Once the idea has been conceived, the next step is to establish whether it is feasible or not. This requires some sort of feasibility study or review

3. Business Case: Assuming the project is feasible, the outline business case should be produced. This will set out the expected benefits, against the likely costs

4. Business Approval: The business then reviews the business case and decide if it is worth proceeding, set against the other things they could do with the money

5. Project Sponsor: If the project is going ahead a senior person in the business needs to sponsor it. They will be responsible to the business for the project's success

6. Project Manager: The first task of the project sponsor is to identify a suitable project manager within the business. If one is not available within the business they may need to recruit one

7. Project Initiation: Finally, once the project manager is in place the project can begin. This first stage of the project is usually referred to as the Initiation Stage

So that's the correct way to start up a project and get the two key players, the project sponsor and project manager in place. In the next topic we look at their roles and the roles of the other people who may be involved in the project.

Assembling the Team

Before anything else can be done on a project, a project manager and a project sponsor need to be appointed. That may seem obvious but it is not always the case.

The Project Manager

We defined the role of the project manager in chapter one but one key aspect to mention under this heading is that it should be a formal appointment. This demonstrates that their role is important to the organization. It also means that everyone else in the organization knows who to talk to if they have a concern or some input to the project. So that's the project manager, now let's move on to the next key role.

The Project Sponsor

The project manager needs someone to talk to who has the business authority to make decisions and commit the money and other resources needed for the project. That person is the project sponsor. Hopefully, they have already identified themselves as the person sanctioning the project. If not, it is important to get an appropriate project sponsor appointed.

The sponsor should operate at a senior level of the business (typically a director or executive) as they will need to justify the project's costs and benefits and 'sell' it to the rest of the business.

The project sponsor is responsible to the business for the viability or justification for the project while the project manager's job is to carry out the project. Therefore the project manager must report to the project sponsor and the sponsor must give the project manager the authority and responsibility for carrying out the project, while maintaining a level of control. The following diagram illustrates their relationship.

Beware

The project manager is often asked to justify the project. Be careful as that should be the sponsor's role.

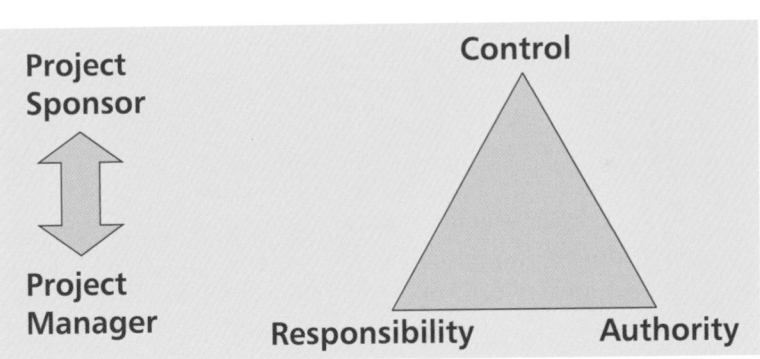

Once the working relationship between the project sponsor and project manager has been established, they can jointly decide on the required composition of the remainder of the project team.

The size and make up of the project team will depend on the size of the project. There is no point in having a large team for a small project, as it will just slow things down. On the other hand a strategic project had better involve representatives of all parts of the business.

Project Stakeholders

The project manager and project sponsor are just two of the many project stakeholders or people with a vested interest in the outcome of a project. We can split stakeholders into three broad groups: the business, the users and the suppliers.

The Business

We have already established that it is the project sponsor's role to represent the business on the project and the project to the business. So the business interests are covered.

The Users

The users are the people who will use or operate whatever it is that the project is implementing. We don't just want to consult them (although that would be an improvement on some projects), we want to involve them on the project. They are the ones who know how the business works and they will use any new product.

The Suppliers

The suppliers are the people, internal or external, who will do the work or provide some input to the project. Typically this could include human resources, accounts, sales, information technology and any other internal or external suppliers who will do any of the work of the project. At the end of the day they are the people who will make the project work.

All three of these stakeholder groups have a vested interest in the outcome of the project and therefore need to be represented on the project team. So the potential composition of the project team is: the project manger, project sponsor, representatives of the people who will use or operate the new product or process and the people who will be doing the work to help to create it. We will look at structuring the project team next.

Beware

Although all three groups have a vested interest it is not always the same interest.

Hot tip

Although you may have several suppliers to involve, they may not all need to be involved at the same time.

The Project Organization

So far we have discussed the roles and skills that we want on the project, although we haven't necessarily identified the actual people yet. The organization of these roles splits into two groups: a steering or supervisory group (usually called the Steering Committee or Project Board) and the actual group who will do the work of the project (usually called the Project Team).

Steering Committee

For a large organization or a complex project the steering committee or project board should consist of: a business executive (the project sponsor); one or more senior users (representing the groups of people who will be using or operating the new product or process); and one or more senior suppliers (representing the people who are doing the work on the project).

The steering committee or project board has three key responsibilities (which are also the responsibility of the three key members): to make sure there is a business case for the project (project sponsor); to make sure it will deliver a solution that can be used (senior user); and to make sure it is technically feasible to do it (senior supplier).

In a small organization or for a small project two or even all three of these roles may be performed by the same person. The steering committee or project board might just be the project sponsor. But in this case the project sponsor is still representing three distinct business functions and still has the above responsibilities.

Project Team

As well as deciding on the size, structure and potential composition of the project board, the project team composition and structure will also need to be defined. Again representatives of all the interested parties need to be included along with any other skills or knowledge that will be required to carry out the project. Asking for specific skills or experience in team members (particularly to fill any gaps in their own knowledge) is not a sign of weakness on the project manager's part, it's a sign of maturity. By doing so they will strengthen the project and that should be their primary concern.

In addition to the steering committee or project board and the project team there may, particularly in larger organizations, be other groups involved.

These other groups could include corporate or programme management, project assurance, quality assurance and project office or project support. Additionally in a very large project the project team itself could be split into a number of smaller teams with their own team managers. The complete project organization could look something like the following diagram.

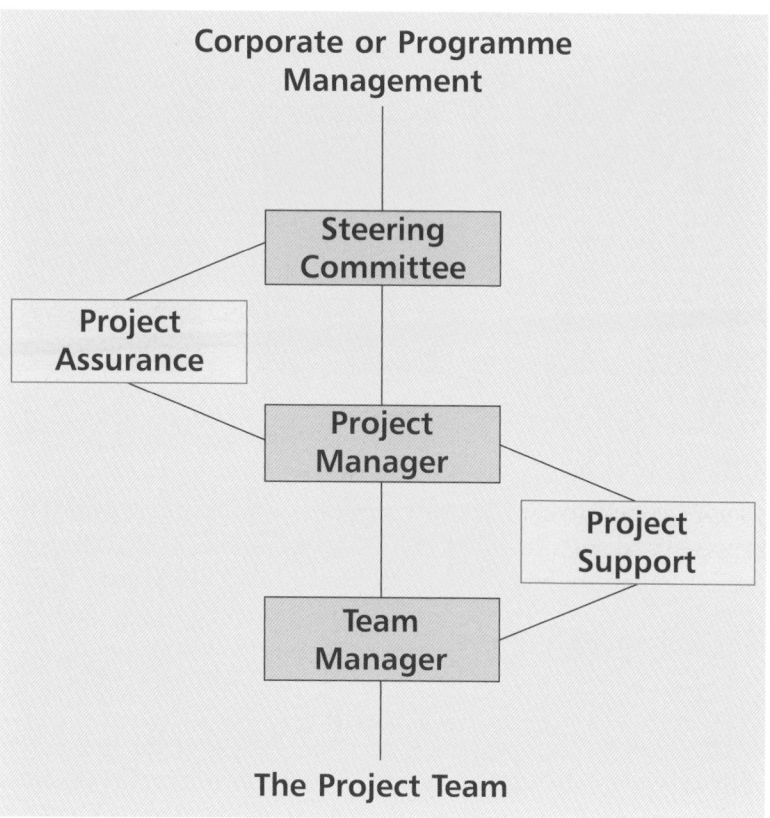

The type of project management structure illustrated above would apply to a large project in a large organization. A smaller project in a smaller organization would just consist of the steering committee, project manager and project team. A medium sized project or organization would be somewhere in between.

But large or small, once the project management structure has been agreed, it should be documented. Then the appropriate people can be approached, their agreement sought to joining the project and the project organization can be finalized.

Why Projects Go Wrong

Successful project management is about completing a project on time, within budget and with the needs of the business fully met. While this is easy to say, a large percentage of projects fail. The most commonly quoted figure is around half of all projects, although, depending on how you define failure, it could be as little as 25% (total failure) or as much as 75% (failed or seriously challenged).

Only around one quarter of projects are completed successfully (within their time, cost and scope targets). In order to get most projects completed, corners are cut, things still take longer than expected and costs increase. But the major factors contributing to project failure are known and well documented; they are:

Unrealistic Estimates

This is probably the most frequently quoted cause of project failure. We will be looking at the right way to develop estimates in chapter five but for the time being consider this: the larger a piece of work is the more likely we are to underestimate how long it will take. The other problem is that people tend to estimate things based on the assumption that nothing will go wrong, but in the real world that rarely happens.

Fuzzy Objectives

It sounds fairly obvious to say that if you don't know what you are trying to achieve you are very unlikely to achieve it. But that is effectively what you are doing if you start a project with poorly defined objectives. The objectives not only need to be clearly defined, they also need to be written down, understood and agreed by both the project team and the business. Objectives should also be SMART: Strategic, Measurable, Agreed, Realistic & Timed.

Beware

Remember Murphy's First Law: Anything that can go wrong, will go wrong.

Hot tip

We will look at SMART Objectives in chapter five.

Poor Communication Skills

We saw in chapter one that a project manager needs to be a good communicator and this is the reason why: lack of clear communication (poor communication skills) by the project manager is the third most frequent cause cited for project failure.

Changing Objectives

Changing the objectives part way through a project is not only very demoralizing to the project team but it is also likely to seriously damage the project. Changes are not always dramatic, sometimes they can be quite minor, but once changes start to creep in they have a way of propagating. One change leads to another and before you know where you are the project has been knocked off track.

Beware

Watch out for Scope Creep: continuous small changes that can drive a project off the rails.

Lack of Top Management Support

For a project to be successful it needs to have active and visible top management support. If a project lacks this it will have no credibility in the eyes of the business. Projects that fall into this category are often so called "vanity projects" as they are the products of someone's vanity and no-one liked to say no to them.

Poor Leadership

If the project manager does not give a strong clear lead or lacks basic leadership skills, then the project is likely to drift. The team won't know what they are supposed to be doing or even worse they won't care.

Lack of Ownership

We defined the project stakeholders as people with a vested interest in the outcome of the project. But if those stakeholders do not accept ownership of the project they will be dealing it the kiss of death.

Poorly Defined Responsibilities

If the project team don't know what their responsibilities are then how can we expect them to carry out their roles? And yet this is cited as a cause of failure in around 50% of failed projects.

Hot tip

Deal with these problems and your project won't go wrong. We'll show you how in the next topic.

Lack of Resources

Finally, failing to identify the required resources or they're not being available when needed is another frequently cited cause of project failure. If you don't have the people the project won't happen.

Getting it Right

Having looked at the most common reasons for project failure in the previous topic, we can build on that and look at how we can make sure the project goes well. These are the key factors:

Clearly Defined Objectives

Before doing anything else make sure the project has clearly defined objectives. Document them and get your project sponsor to agree them on behalf of the business. Then when you assemble the project team the first time, explain the objectives to them and get their agreement as well.

Good Communications

If you have any concerns about your communications skills get yourself on a communications course or buy a book on it. The more you communicate the easier it gets. We will be looking at communications in more detail in chapter eight, but for now consider creating a communications plan: setting out who you will communicate with, how you will do it and how often.

Realistic Budget and Resources

For a project to be successful you need to have an adequate and realistic budget together with the human and other resources to carry it out. So at the start of the project identify what financial and human resources you will need and ask for them.

Commitment to the Project

The project manager, the project sponsor, the project team and all the stakeholders need to be committed to the project for it to be successful. How do you make sure you get that commitment? By asking for it and that is back to communication again.

Hot tip

We will look at defining objectives in more detail in chapter five.

30

Realistic Planning

Planning is the most important skill for a project manager. So start out by developing a realistic and achievable plan. That means allowing time for the things you don't know about as well as the things you do know about. We will be looking at the right way to develop a plan in chapter four.

Competent Team

Once you have defined the resources you will need to carry out the project you need to select the people with the right skills and knowledge to fulfill the roles. You will be asking for people from other parts of the business to be assigned to your project team and you need someone senior to authorize it.

Top Management Support

This is where your project sponsor comes in. They represent the business to the project and they also need to represent the project to the business. Make sure they demonstrate their commitment to the project by promoting it to the rest of the business.

End User Buy In

The end users, the people whose jobs will be impacted by the project, all too often get forgotten. Don't rely on their managers telling them what is going on, go and talk to them yourself. Your communications plan should include the end users. By talking to them and listening to them you will be able to get their buy in, which is essential for the success of the project.

Defined Milestones

Defined and regular milestones are the way that you measure the progress of the project. They should represent significant events in the life of the project and they should be defined as part of the plan. Then, as each is reached, you can ask yourself if the project is on track and if not initiate corrective action.

Regular Monitoring

Finally, regular monitoring and progress tracking is essential if your project is going to be successful. So right from the outset define how you are going to track progress, how you will measure it and how you will report on it.

Use these ten factors as a checklist during project start up. If you can tick all ten boxes then your project is going to go well.

Hot tip

Ask 'up front' for any skills and people you need. It's a lot easier than trying to get them later.

31

Terms of Reference

Once the project organization, structure and composition have been agreed, any other project information can be consolidated to produce terms of reference for the project. This document (sometimes referred to as the Project Brief or Statement of Work) brings together all the background to the project.

Project Mandate

To start with there may have been some form of mandate or authorization to begin the project. Ideally, it will be a formal board minute, written request from a director or some form of a feasibility study recommendation with senior management approval. In practice it is just as likely to be a scribbled note or 'someone in authority' asking you to do it.

Terms of Reference

Whatever sort of mandate the project is starting from, it needs to be turned into proper terms of reference, that can be used, by the business to authorize the project to start. Create the terms of reference by carrying out these steps:

1. Define the project: including any background, objectives, scope and constraints

2. Outline the Business Case: the justification for carrying out the project

3. Document the customers' quality expectations: which will determine the overall quality of the project's deliverables

4. Define the acceptance criteria: what the business will want to see in order to accept the results

5. List any known risks which could impact on the project or the business

This becomes a formal document, which you present to the business, in order to confirm that the business is happy for the project to start.

There is an example terms of reference opposite and in the next topic we will go through the steps of preparing one.

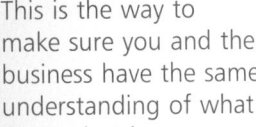

Hot tip

This is the way to make sure you and the business have the same understanding of what the project is.

Background

Bill's Bike Shop is a small business owned and run by Bill Bounce with a staff of six. Bill would like to develop a cycle touring holiday 'product' in the South West and preliminary costings indicates it should be viable.

Project Objectives

To design and introduce the South West Tours product, based on the provision of bicycle hire and holiday accommodation. The product needs to be launched in time for next season's peak booking time (new year). The product will be launched and will operate within budgets (once agreed).

The desired outcome is an operational holiday business and the key deliverables from the project are a holiday brochure; operational infrastructure to run the business; agreements with accommodation suppliers; and the availability of hire cycles. Any external expenditure must be budgeted and agreed in advance.

Outline Business Case

The project will support business strategy by introducing a new product that uses and encourages bicycle riding in the South West. It is also expected that the product itself will produce a positive revenue stream in its own right once established.

Quality Expectations

The customer wants the product to be seen as a quality holiday product rather than a cheap holiday product. The literature and organization introduced must therefore support this image and all processes and agreements must be fully documented to allow ongoing support following hand over of the product.

Acceptance Criteria

For the customer to accept the final product and key interim deliverables, they will need to be seen as 'Quality' products that are fit for their intended purpose. They must also be fully supportable by the business.

Known Risks

There have been no major risks identified by the customer.

Creating the Terms of Reference

The first stage in preparing the Terms of Reference is to gather the information for the project definition. If you have a Project Mandate a lot of this information will be included there, if not it will need to be gathered.

Project Definition

The project definition states what is to be done in the project. You should document any of the following information that is relevant to the project:

1   Background Information: note down any information about previous projects or feasibility studies that have been carried out together with any other historical information that could have a bearing on the project

2   Objectives: state what the project has to achieve and what will need to be produced by it. It does not need to say why the project is being carried out as that should be in the background information

3   Scope: define what is included (needs) in the project and any boundaries (or limitations)

4   Deliverables: list the tangible things that the project will need to produce (this will build on the objectives)

5   Exclusions: the scope defines what is in the project, in this section specify anything that is excluded from it

6   Constraints: detail any restrictions or limits on the way the project can be run

7   Interfaces: list any other projects or events which could have an impact on (or could be impacted by) this project

Once you have completed the project definition you should get it reviewed by the project sponsor as they may be aware of other information that should also be included. Once you are happy with the definition, carry on with the other sections as follows.

The Outline Business Case

This is the strategic or high-level justification for carrying out the project. It should spell out how the project will support the business strategy or plans. It should contain any feasibility study findings together with a justification of the reasons for this particular approach to solving the business opportunity or problem.

As previously noted, the project manager should not be the person who has to make the Business Case. It should have already been made by the business and preferably as a result of a feasibility study. We will look at the Business Case in more detail in chapter three.

Customers' Quality Expectations

This should define what is really important about the deliverables or results of the project. Is it to be a 'quick and dirty' fix for a time critical problem or is a 'quality solution' required that would be usable and maintainable for years to come? Whatever the expectations, they should be stated.

Acceptance Criteria

This is a definition of what must be done for the final product to be acceptable to the customer and end-user staff who will be affected. These should relate to the quality expectations and could include target dates, functionality, appearance, performance levels, capacity, availability, cost, security, ease of use or timings. They should include some form of measurements so that the success of the project can be properly ascertained.

Known Risks

Although a detailed risk analysis will be carried out later, any known risks should be documented as they will form part of the decision on whether the project should go ahead or not.

Finally before we go to the business for the decision to proceed, we need to start planning for the first stage of the project, the Initiation Stage. We will look at how to do that in the next topic.

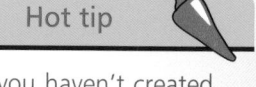

Project Planning

The final step in starting up a project is to produce a plan for the first stage of the project. This is traditionally called the Initiation Stage (or sometimes the Planning Stage). The reason for only planning the first stage of the project at this time is that the full project plan is one of the things produced during the Initiation Stage (which is why it is sometimes referred to as the Planning Stage).

The reason for needing a plan for the Initiation Stage is that you are going to ask the business to authorize it (and the resources required to carry it out), based on the project's Terms of Reference.

Planning is covered in more detail in chapter four and the Initiation Stage is covered in chapter ten, but you may like to have an initial go at producing a draft Initiation Stage plan based on what you already know about your project.

Preparing the Plan

The first step in producing a stage plan is to list out the tasks that need to be carried out and the deliverables that will need to be produced. The following is a list of typical Initiation Stage tasks with their associated deliverables:

1. Schedule and hold the initial team meeting, obtain agreement to the project objectives and issue minutes

2. Set up the required project information and filing systems and issue project filing policy

3. Agree project reporting structure and document it

4. Produce the initial (outline) project plan and the detailed plan for next stage of the project

5. Review and refine the business case and risks based on the plan

Assemble the Project Initiation Document (an updated version of the Terms of Reference), present it to management and obtain approval to proceed.

Review the list of Tasks and associated Deliverables for your project and make any changes or add additional Tasks or Deliverables that you have identified and list them on a schedule form like the one below.

Task	01	02	03	04	05	06	07	08	09	10	11	12	13	14	15
Organize Team Meeting (1 day)	■														
Set up Information and Systems (1 day)		■													
Agree Reporting Structure (1 day)			■												
Produce Outline Plan (2 days)				■											
Review Business Case and Risks (1 day)							■								
Hold Kick-off Team Meeting (1 day)									■						
Document the Results (1 day)										■					
Review with Sponsor (1 Day)											■				

Hot tip

This is only a part of a typical planning chart, when you draw it up you should make it much wider.

Now estimate the likely person/days work effort for each Task and write them in under the description of the task as shown on the form above.

When you have done that plot in a schedule on the right-hand side of the form by shading in a line for how long (the duration) each Task will take to complete. This type of chart is called a Gantt chart. If you get to the right-hand side before you've finished, wrap round and start from the left again. Don't worry too much about technique for now as we will spend more time on planning, estimating and scheduling later in the book.

The Initiation Stage is typically a short stage and the Tasks involved are usually quite short, so it is usual to schedule it on a low-level Gantt Chart (showing days rather than weeks or months).

What Next?
Once the Initiation Stage has been planned, formal approval to begin it (based on the Terms of Reference) can be sought and the project proper started. The decision on whether to approve the Initiation Stage should be based on the outline business case and the initiation stage plan.

Beware

No matter how much pressure you are put under, do not skip the Initiation Stage, you'll see why later.

Summary

- You only ever get one chance to start each project, so make sure you start it right

- Even if your project has already started, use this chapter as a checklist and back fill anything you may have missed

- The steps involved in starting a project are: conceive the idea; establish the feasibility; develop the outline business case; obtain business approval; appoint a project sponsor; appoint a project manager; then initiate the project

- As well as the project manager and project sponsor, identify the other project stakeholders and make sure they are represented in the project team

- Define the required project management structure in keeping with the size of the project and the size of the organization

- Be aware of what can go wrong on a project during project start up and avoid unrealistic estimates; fuzzy objectives; poor communications; changing objectives; lack of top management support; poor leadership; lack of ownership; poorly defined responsibilities; and lack of resources

- Be aware of what can make a project go right during project start up and use this as a checklist for your project

- Develop your project's Terms of Reference covering: the project definition; the outline business case; the customers' quality expectations; the acceptance criteria; and document any known risks

- Don't try to plan the entire project too soon, you will not have enough information at the start

- Start the project planning process by developing the tasks and deliverables for your project Initiation Stage

- Schedule the initiation stage on a simple Gantt chart showing when each task will take place and how long it will take to complete

- Take your Terms of Reference and Initiation Stage Plan to the business and request formal authority to begin the project

3 The Business Case

The Business Case sets out the justification for the project. It is fundamental to a successful project and this chapter shows you how to develop it.

Feasibility

Ideally the project will have been preceded by some form of feasibility study, which will have established that it is worth proceeding with the project. But if a feasibility study has not previously been carried out, then the project manager will need to establish and agree the feasibility of the project with the sponsor (in effect carrying out the feasibility study) during the project start up and before the project formally begins. The steps that need to be taken to do this are:

1 Start out by defining the reasons for carrying out the project and establish the benefits that the business expects to gain from it

2 Then find out if the project is right for the organization; is it happening at the right time and is it in line with the mission and strategic objectives of the business?

3 Assuming the results of the first two steps are positive, now consider what the likely costs of the project will be in terms of financial costs and also the demands on human resources

4 Next consider if there are any business risks associated with carrying out the project

5 Finally ask yourself if the project has a senior business champion, someone who is pushing for the project and can make the decision to allocate resources to it

Beware

Never lose sight of the business strategy and how the project supports it. It is the reason for the project.

Once you have carried out these five steps you have performed a feasibility study. You can now weigh the possible benefits to the business against the likely costs and risks to the business of carrying out the project. If the business decides, in the light of this information, that they wish to go ahead with the project, you have established the outline business case.

The Business Case explains, in business terms, why the project is being carried out. It states the business benefits that are expected to flow from the project together with the costs of the project and how they will be incurred.

Outline Business Case

What we have just been doing in establishing the initial feasibility of the project is defining the outline business case. This represents the initial, high level, justification for the cost of carrying out the project. It should describe how the project will support the business strategy and indicate the reasons why this particular approach is being proposed for the business requirements or problem.

Developing the Business Case

The initial outline business case will, of necessity, only be based on a rough idea of what the project is likely to cost and an outline idea of the likely benefits that will flow from it.

During the course of the project, more information about costs will become available. First about the projected costs and then the actual costs. Likewise more information will become available about the expected benefits.

The Business Case, therefore, needs to be a living document that evolves over time. In order to make sure this happens, the Business Case needs to be reviewed at regular intervals. Then, if the costs appear to exceed the benefits at any time, the project should be reviewed and if necessary stopped.

Initiation Stage

One of the main reasons for adding an Initiation Stage to the project, is to spend a little more time confirming what the project will involve and producing realistic cost estimates. These will then be used to refine and develop the business case.

The Business Case

The information for the Business Case comes from a number of sources including: the Project Mandate, the Terms of Reference, the Project Plan (however outline it is at this stage); and from the business itself.

Documenting the Business Case

An example business case is set out on the page opposite. Based on whatever available information you have gathered from the above (and any other) sources you have available, carry out the following steps:

1 Edit the standard purpose of the document to suit your own organization and the level of detail on which you are basing the document

2 Fill in the reasons for the project. These will either be in the project mandate or terms of reference or you will have established them in the feasibility exercise

3 List all the benefits that have been identified. This should include financial and non-financial, and quantifiable and no-quantifiable benefits. Many organizations now include environmental benefits as well

4 Under benefits realization describe how the quantifiable financial benefits will start to accrue

5 Under costs and time scale, list the projected costs of carrying out the project and the ongoing costs of operating the new process or system. Clearly if there are ongoing costs there may also be ongoing savings, which should be included above

6 Finally under investment appraisal give the overall picture using something like a discounted cash flow model. We will look at these later in the chapter

When the Business Case is complete it should be reviewed and agreed, first with the project team (to confirm it can be achieved) and then with the business (who must accept ownership of it).

Hot tip

Remember: although the project manager may assemble the business case it is owned by the business.

Example Business Case

Purpose of the Document
To document the justification for undertaking a project based on the estimated cost and the anticipated business benefits to be gained. The project sponsor will monitor the ongoing viability of the project against this business case.

Reasons
The project will support business strategy by introducing a new product that uses and encourages bicycle riding in the West Country. It is also expected to produce a positive revenue stream once established.

Benefits
Based on initial projections, the product is forecast to achieve sales of $50,000 and a gross profit of $25,000 in the first full year of operation. With annual operating costs forecast at $15,000 this will result in a net profit to the business of $10,000 per annum. It will also increase the turnover of bicycles through the main business.

Benefits Realization
There will be no benefits during the development year (year 0) with $10,000 per annum from year 1 onwards.

Cost and Time scale
The one-off project costs will be $15,000 all in year 0 and the annual operating costs will be $15,000 from year 1 onwards.

Investment Appraisal
In the following table Discounted Cash Flow is calculated at 8% per annum. It will be seen that payback starts in year 1 and the cash flow becomes positive in year 2.

	Year 0	Year 1	Year 2	Year 3
Sales	0	50,000	50,000	50,000
Cost of Sales	0	25,000	25,000	25,000
Operation	15,000	15,000	15,000	15,000
Profit (Loss)	(15,000)	10,000	10,000	10,000
DCF	(15,000)	9,200	8,464	7,787
Cumulative	(15,000)	(5,800)	2,664	10,451

Hot tip

It is always a good idea to state the purpose of a document, you may know what it's for but others might not.

Developing the Costs

One of the first questions a project manager gets asked is "How much is all this going to cost?" and it's usually only moments after being 'given' the project in the first place!

No-one can be expected to produce a reliable cost estimate until they have a full grasp of the business requirements. This will only be available two stages into the project. So, anything produced before then should be clearly identified as a preliminary estimate and issued with a corresponding 'health warning'.

Experts

The people within a business who are best able to produce accurate cost estimates will normally reside in a Finance or Accounts section. Using them should not only save the project manager a lot of time, but should also ensure the accuracy of the figures. Some organizations will allocate a finance person to each project as a project accountant. If not here is a guide to developing project costs.

Costing

Take the internal people work effort estimates and cost them up. Then add any other internal or external one-off costs (the costs of the project). Then add any recurring costs (the ongoing costs of operating the new product). Let's look at each of these in turn:

Internal People Costs

If the business operates on a cost center principle, or charges clients for people's time it may already have internal charging rates. If not, they can be calculated.

Take the average annual salary for each grade of person working on the project and double it (to allow for premises and all the other costs of running the business). Then divide it by 180 (this will be explained in scheduling) to get a daily internal cost. It is probably a good idea to check this figure with you finance people to see if they can come up with anything better.

This daily internal cost rate can then be used to cost up the time each team member is estimated to spend on the project to give the total internal people cost.

External People Costs

External people working on a project will be charging for their time in some way. It may be a fixed cost for providing a service or it may be on a daily or hourly rate. Whatever it is can be used as the external people cost.

Other Project Costs

These could include costs for a project office, furniture, computers, telephones, secretarial services, etc. There may be software costs such as a Project Scheduler and there may be a need to include travel, training or other appropriate costs.

Capital Costs

The costs of computer or other equipment, software packages or development, operating systems or database costs will normally be treated as capital (although the business may lease them). The relevant suppliers (or potential suppliers) should provide all of these costs.

The business will have a standard way of treating capital, dependent on whether they lease or purchase and how they choose to depreciate and write it off. Again your finance or accounts department should be able to help with this.

Revenue Operating Costs

Finally the ongoing or operating costs of the new product need to be determined for its expected life time. The annual charge for the capital costs will be determined by the business (see above). The other operating costs will need to be calculated.

These could include staff (additional people to operate the new product), annual maintenance or support costs for hardware (computer or otherwise), annual support or maintenance for software, operating systems, database licences, insurance and any other recurring costs that are generated by the results of the project.

Having established the costs of running the project and whatever new process, product or system the project implements, we will look at how to present and assess them in the next topic.

Hot tip

This may not be a complete list, there may be other costs that you should account for.

Investment Appraisal

The Investment Appraisal is the business process of deciding whether or not to carry out a project. In order to appraise the business investment we need to calculate three things:

1 The cost of doing nothing, or what will happen if we do not carry out the project

2 The cost of carrying out the project in terms of the expenditure (finance) and the use of human resources (manpower)

3 The benefits (in financial terms) that will flow from the results of the project if we carry it out

While the project manager needs to calculate the cost of carrying out the project, they should not quantify the cost or benefit implications of doing (or not doing) the project. Either the project sponsor or some other financial or business experts within the business should calculate these.

Ownership

The business case must be 'owned' by the business through the project sponsor, steering committee or project board. The project manager has to stay objective about the project and not end up 'selling' it to the business (unfortunately that seems to happen all too often).

Doing Nothing

People sometimes forget that 'doing nothing' is always an option. So the first step in appraising the business investment is to set out the cost of doing nothing. It may be this that justifies the project by itself. If the cost of doing nothing would be a significant loss of business, heavy maintenance costs or some penalty for noncompliance with a legal requirement, then the cost of doing nothing could well be significant.

The cost of doing nothing needs to be calculated as from the time when, if the project were to be carried out, the new product would be implemented. The cost will continue for what would be the expected life of the new product. This keeps the cost of doing nothing in line with any other alternatives.

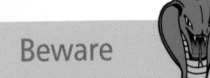

Beware

Do not be tempted to quantify benefits or you will end up owning them.

Hot tip

If you identify any new benefits, tell the business so they can quantify them.

Project Costs

Having calculated the business cost of doing nothing, the business cost of carrying out the project needs to be defined in the same way. This needs to show the cost of carrying out the project and operating the new product. It is usual to set out the cost of the investment over time and this is normally produced in some form of table or spreadsheet. A useful graphical representation of costs is the cumulative cost curve, which shows the cumulative cost on one axis and time on the other.

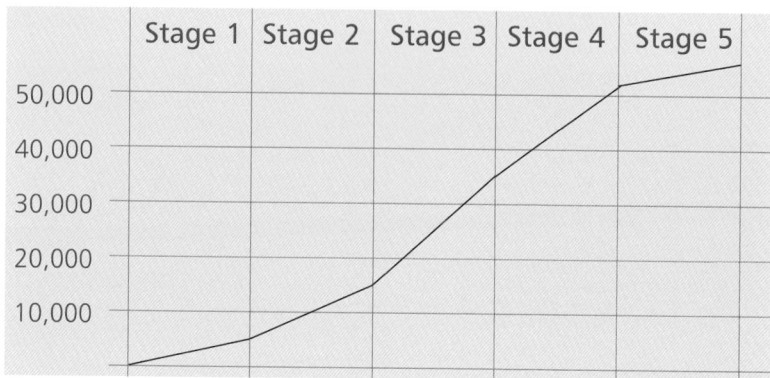

The time axis can be in months or just the undated project stages (as illustrated above). This shows the business the rate at which costs will be incurred and highlights the benefits in taking a controlled approach to the project.

Benefits

The benefits, in terms of reduced costs or increased income over the lifetime of the product, should be calculated by the business. This would include the cost of doing nothing as that is a cost that will be saved by the project. If no direct benefits result from the project, then the project does not have a business case in its own right. It may still be required to enable some other business requirement to be dealt with, but in this case it should be justified by that other requirement. If there is no business case when considered by itself or in conjunction with another project, then the project is not economically viable.

Once the costs and benefits have been calculated, it is usual to set them out in some form of cash flow model. This is covered in the next topic.

Beware

If the project is not economically viable in its own right, then make sure the business knows this.

Cash Flow Model

Having calculated the costs and financial benefits flowing from the project, they need to be set out in a suitable way for the business to appraise the required investment.

Organizational Standards

Most organizations have their own standards for appraising business investments and clearly any organizational standards should be followed. The most common (and the one to use if your organization doesn't have a standard) are cash flow models. These give a good picture of the real impact of a project on the business finances. See the example in the following table:

	Year 0	Year 1	Year 2	Year 3
Benefits	0	30	30	30
Costs	100	10	10	10
Net Benefit	-100	20	20	20
Cash Flow	-100	-80	-60	-40
Discount Factor	1.0	0.95	0.9	0.86
Discounted NB	-100	19	18	17
Discounted CF	-100	-81	-63	-46

This has a time scale that represents the costs of carrying out the project (in year 0) and the expected life of the resultant product (in years 1 to 3). The model is created using the following steps:

1 Enter the annual financial benefits that will flow from the project in each year after the project has been completed (there will be no financial benefit in year 0 unless the project is completed before the end of the year)

2 Enter the cost of carrying out the project in year 0 and the annual cost of operating the resultant process for the number of years it is expected to last

3 Subtract the cost from the benefit and enter the result in the Net Benefit row, this will show what the project will cost or contribute to the business each year

Hot tip

Make sure you stay objective, it is for the business to decide if the investment is justified or not.

4 In the Cash Flow row enter the net benefit for year 0, then for each succeeding year add that year's net benefit to the previous year's cash flow

If the model were extended the cash flow numbers would appear to show that it would break even in year five and start producing a profit from year six onwards. However, this ignores the effect of time on money.

Discounting

Most organizations use some method, such as discounting, so that future costs and benefits are expressed in 'today's money'. The discount factor will normally be dictated by current interest rates and represents the net current value of money. In the example in the table opposite, a discount factor of 5% has been used ($1 today only being worth 95c in one year and so on). Your finance or accounts department will be able to provide this for you.

5 Enter the discount factors that you have been provided or use the example on the left, just reduce each year by a further 5% if you require more years

6 Multiply each years' net benefit by that year's discount factor to give the Discounted Net Benefit (Discounted NB in the table)

7 Finally calculate the Discounted Cash Flow (Discounted CF in the table) in the same way the cash flow was calculated in step 4 above, but this time using the discounted net benefit rather than the net benefit

By assessing a project's discounted cash flow we are allowing for inflation and the value of money over time. In the example shown in the table on the left, the project will not now break even until year six and only start showing a profit in year seven.

Typically a project would need to break even within three years and start showing a profit following that to be considered seriously by the business. So on that basis this project would not now be viable.

Reviewing the Business Case

The outline Business Case will normally be produced either before or during the start up of the project. When the project moves into the Initiation Stage, the Business Case should be reviewed.

Refining the Business Case

The most important activity in the Initiation Stage is planning the project. This will provide the answers to some key questions like how long it will take and how much it is going to cost? These planned costs should be used to refine the business case, replacing the initial estimates of the likely costs.

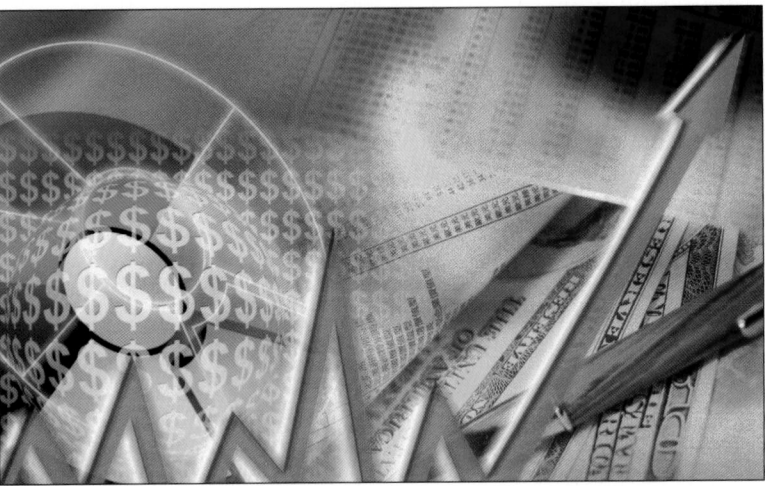

Because the outline business case will normally only be based on a best guess for the costs and benefits, the full business case should be reviewed. The planning process may have uncovered factors that will impact on the benefits or the effective life of the product. In addition to the capital cost of carrying out the project we should also now have a better idea of the ongoing operating costs of the results of the project.

New factors and information about the project and the business case will continue to come to light throughout the project. So we need to review the business case at regular intervals and we can do this through the stage review process.

Stage Reviews

Stage reviews provide the opportunity for the project sponsor and the business to satisfy themselves that the project is being well run by the project manager. We will be looking at stage reviews later in the book but the key factor is that they will include a review of the business case based on the actual costs to date plus the estimated costs to completion. At each subsequent stage we will know more about the actual cost.

Project Review

At the end of the project we will have the actual cost of the project so we can review the business case in the light of the real cost. However, we will not yet know what the real benefits to the business are as they will take some time to come through. For this reason it is usual to plan a post-project review several months after the end of the project when the final review of the business case can be made based on the real costs and the real benefits.

There are other times when the business case should be reviewed: such as when we consider making a change to the project or when a project issue occurs.

Change Requests

We will be looking at change control later in the book but part of that process is reviewing the business case. The first question to be asked is: if we make this change to the project, what impact will it have on the business case? The second question is: if we do not make the change will it have an impact on the business case? If there is any impact either way, then the project sponsor needs to be appraised of the fact so that the appropriate business decision can be made.

Project Issues

The project manager is responsible for keeping the project sponsor aware of any issues that arise in the project. Issues will often have an impact on the business case if they involve delays or increased costs and they frequently do.

In return the project sponsor must keep the project manager aware of any issues that arise in the business that could impact on the project's business case. A strategic change in the business might even negate the reasons for a project.

So, in addition to the formal reviews at the end of each project stage, the project manager and project sponsor must monitor the business case on an ongoing basis.

Hot tip

Never lose sight of the business case, it's why you are carrying out the project.

Summary

- Before starting a project its feasibility should be established through a feasibility study; if that hasn't happened the project manager should do it retrospectively

- Once the project's feasibility has been established the outline business case should be developed, setting out the likely costs of the project and the expected benefits

- The business case should set out the reasons for carrying out the project; the expected benefits and the way in which they will be realized; the costs and time scale for the project and the ongoing operating costs; and some form of investment appraisal

- While the project manager should not be the person to estimate the benefits of the project, they are the person who should be responsible for developing the costs of the project

- Project costs should include internal people costs, external people costs, the capital costs of any purchases, training costs, and the ongoing operating or revenue costs

- Once the costs of the project have been developed an investment appraisal can be carried out setting out the benefits against the cost of the project and the appraisal should always consider the potential cost of doing nothing

- The investment appraisal should include some form of cash flow model setting out the way that money will be spent and recovered; it should also take into account the value of money over time

- The business case should be refined and reviewed at the end of the Initiation Stage and as part of the review of each subsequent stage

- The business case should also be reviewed when considering any changes to the project and when considering the impact of any project issues

- The final review of the business case should take place some time after the end of the project so that not only can the real costs be reflected but also the real benefits

4 Planning

Planning a project is one of the most critical tasks that a project manager does. This chapter will show you how to develop an effective project plan.

Objectives

Before starting to develop any type of plan, it is essential to have a clear statement of the objectives (what it is that the plan is to achieve).

Business Objectives

The objectives must define, in business terms, the strategy they are addressing as well as the aims for the project. Then they can become a focus for the project team and the business. They will help to ensure that the business understands what the project team is doing, focus the project team on the correct target, create commitment to and agreement about the project objectives and ensure that all interested parties are involved in achieving a successful project outcome.

Hot tip

Make sure you have clear, agreed objectives before you start planning.

SMART Objectives

A useful acronym for Objectives is they should be SMART: Strategic, Measurable, Agreed, Realistic and Timed.

Strategic

Objectives must address a strategic business need. Vague objectives such as 'improve customer satisfaction' or 'reduce stock levels' are all very well, but what is the underlying business strategy? What strategic goal does the business want to achieve and what is this project doing to help reach it? If the business objective is to be the largest supplier in a market place, then the strategy could be to provide the best after sales service, or perhaps to process orders faster than the competition. In the latter case, the project objectives could be to introduce a new system or process that will allow orders to be taken, processed, dispatched and delivered to the customer within 24 hours. This is a clear step towards achieving the strategic business objective.

Measurable

If the objective can't be measured, there will be no way of knowing if it's been achieved. Yet, in many projects, the new product is never measured (perhaps to avoid embarrassment). If a new process is to speed things up, how much should it speed things up by? Reducing a process turn round time from 48 hours to 24 hours is measurable, a 25% reduction in stock levels is measurable, even improved cash flow can be measured.

Agreed

If the objectives are not agreed by the business, users and suppliers the project will be destined to fail. Clearly, the business must agree that it is what they want from the project, and also what they are prepared to pay for. It stands to reason that everyone on the project team must agree with them, or they will have no motivation to achieve them. The suppliers and customers (internal or external) must agree with the objectives if they are going to be impacted by them. In other words, everyone touched by the project should understand and agree the objectives.

Hot tip

It is worth getting all your stakeholders to review and agree the objectives.

Realistic

If the objectives are not realistic, the project team will soon realize and start to lose commitment. There is no point in having objectives that can't be achieved. Either they will be ignored or, worse still, they will actually demotivate the team. "Everyone knew we could never achieve it" or "It was all pie in the sky" are typical quotes from failed projects. If everyone knew that why didn't they kill the project?

Beware

If the objectives are not realistic, they will demotivate the team.

Timed

Finally the objectives must be timed. If there is no time scale, there will be no pressure to achieve it. The period in which the objectives are to be met needs to be defined (e.g. 'the increase in productivity should be delivered within one year'). The time scale needs to be realistic, as new products and processes take time to settle in and get fully up to speed.

If a Business Objective can satisfy these five criteria, then it is a real objective and the business and project team should be committed to it. The following example is an illustration of a typical SMART objective.

South West Tours

To design and introduce the new holiday product based on the provision of bicycle hire and holiday accommodation. The product needs to be launched in time for next season's peak booking time (new year). The product will be launched and will operate within the agreed budget for the first year.

Constraints

Having first defined the objectives of the project, the next step is to define the constraints. These are the things that can restrict or limit the project in some way. They would typically include things like the amount of money that is available for the budget, the time the project has to be completed in and the human resources that the business can allocate to work on it. They could also include things like standards and procedures that have to be followed.

Identifying Constraints

In order to identify the constraints that apply to your project you will need to speak to people in the business and possibly external bodies for advice on standards. Start by speaking to your project sponsor first and then ask him or her who else they think you need to speak to.

Use the following steps to determine the constraints:

Hot tip

Don't make any commitments until you are sure you can achieve them.

1   What time frame does the project need to be completed in? Is there some compelling business need for it to be ready by a critical date or is it just nice to have? But don't forget at this stage you won't yet know if it is achievable in the required time frame so don't make any commitments to meeting it, that will come later

2   What budget is available and what restrictions will be placed on it? Again you won't yet know how much it is all going to cost, you are just finding out what the business believes it can afford to spend on it. The business might also want you to request the budget in several slices so that they can satisfy themselves it is still justified

3   What human resources will you be able to call on to carry out the project? If the project is large these will ideally be allocated to the project on a full-time basis but more usually they will be on a part-time basis and often there will be a limitation on how many people the business can spare

4   What other resources will the business make available for you to call on? This could include an office for you and

the team to work in, computers and other equipment, information and raw materials

5 What constraints will apply to the results of the project? This might include a target price, size or weight if the project is to develop a new product

6 What organizational, quality or compliance standards does the project have to comply with? Many large organizations will have some sort of project management standards in place. Any manufacturing organization will have quality and health and safety standards that must be complied with. Financial organizations and food and drug manufacturers will have compliance regulations that have to be followed and maybe even audited

The initial answers you receive to the questions might be very clear but they are more likely to be vague to begin with. You need to be persistent in getting clarification and if the project sponsor or whoever it is you are asking can't give you a clear answer ask them who you should speak to in order to clarify it. Then repeat the process with that person.

Once you have received clear answers to these questions you will need to document the constraints so that you can get the business to agree them. A typical statement of constraints could look like the following.

Hot tip

Be persistent in your questioning until you get a clear answer.

57

Project Constraints

- It is critical that the project is completed in time for the start of the new business year on January 1

- The project will operate within a maximum budget of $100,000, which will be allocated stage by stage

- The equivalent of three full-time people will be allocated to the project for six months

- The project will be carried out in full compliance with the organization's project management, quality and health and safety standards and regulations

Starting the Plan

Having defined the project's objectives and constraints we can now begin the planning process by defining what the project will have to produce to meet its objectives. The best place to start that process is at the end.

Start at the End

We defined a project as having a beginning, a middle and an end. When producing project plans start at the end (what the project is setting out to achieve). This is the product which the project is delivering, it is the major project deliverable. It's the thing that will address the business need. But, while there may be just one major deliverable, the new product, process or state, there will usually be many interim deliverables as well. We need to identify them as well as the final product.

Work Back to the Beginning

So work your way back from the final deliverables to the start of the project identifying all of the things that the project is going to produce along the way, its deliverables.

When you have done that, start your preliminary project plan using the following steps:

1 Write down a brief summary of your project objectives at the top of a sheet of paper

2 Next list the main deliverables from the project, the final product and all the interim deliverables that you have identified down the left-hand side of the page, in the sequence in which they will need to be produced

3 Now to the right of each deliverable, list the work that will need to be done to produce it. It may just be one task, but it is more likely to be several

This is the start of the project plan. There will normally be more tasks or activities on the right-hand side than there are deliverables on the left.

The example on the page opposite works back from having the new product operational, to designing it, selecting suppliers, agreeing the business requirements to planning the project.

Don't forget

Make sure you have SMART objectives then start planning by identifying your deliverables.

South West Tours

To design and introduce the new holiday product based on the provision of bicycle hire and holiday accommodation. The product needs to be launched in time for next season's peak booking time (New Year). The product will be launched and will operate within the agreed budget for the first year.

Key Deliverable	Tasks
Project Plan	Plan the project
Project Initiation Document (PID)	Review the business case Write the PID
Business Requirements	Interview & information gathering Document requirements Obtain business agreement
Requirements Specification	Review competing products Define detailed requirements Develop initial implementation strategy
Suppliers Selected	Identify potential suppliers Negotiate and appoint
Product Design	Refine requirements Produce draft designs Agree with the business
Implementation Strategy	Develop test & acceptance plans Prepare staff training plan Agree implementation strategy
Agreed Products	Agree designs and schedules Review and agree final products
Operational Documentation	Develop user and other documentation
New Product Launched	Place advertisements Train staff Introduce new systems
New Product Operational	Provide support for initial period Hand over project documentation
End Project Report	Produce end project report Close project

Hot tip

As you start to list the deliverables and tasks you will keep thinking of more, just keep adding them in.

59

Beware

This is not a complete plan, it is a typical preliminary project plan.

Structuring the Plan

In Chapter one we defined a project as having a beginning, a middle and an end. We then expanded that into a simple, four-step approach to carrying out a project, which we could also use for structuring our plan. But in fact it is not quite right yet, we can develop it a little more:

1 Define the Objectives: needs to be broadened so that it becomes the Initiation Stage

2 Plan the Project: also moves into the Initiation Stage so we will replace it with two new stages: the Strategy Stage and the Analysis Stage

3 Carry it Out: then becomes stage four which we will call the Design & Build Stage.

4 Hand it Over: becomes stage five which we will call the Implementation Stage. So let's define what each of these project stages will actually do.

Five Stage Approach

This gives us five project stages or five steps to carrying out a project as follows:

1 Initiation Stage: to start the project up by confirming the business case and developing the project plan

2 Strategy Stage: to gather details of the business requirements, document them and agree them with the business

3 Analysis Stage: to work out what will have to be done in order to meet the business requirements

4 Design & Build Stage: to work out how we are going to do what needs to be done and then do it (build it, buy it or carry it out)

5 Implementation Stage: to implement it and hand it over

Each stage builds logically on what has been done in the previous stage and we have also identified some more project deliverables and added them in. If we take our key deliverables we can now list them under the appropriate project stage and add any others:

Stage	Deliverables
Initiation	Business Case Project Plan Project Initiation Document End Stage Report
Strategy	Business Requirements End Stage Report
Analysis	Requirements Specification Suppliers Selected Product Definition End Stage Report
Design & Build	Product Design Implementation Strategy Training Plan Agreed Products Brochures & Other Material Operational Documentation Advertising Booked End Stage Report
Implementation	Staff Training Advertising New Product Launched New Product Operational End Project Report

We have also added end stage reports to mark these key milestones to the business.

Not every project will necessarily need all five stages. In theory a short project, with well defined objectives and requirements, could consist of just three stages: Initiation, Design & Build and Implementation. A longer project might need more than five stages, but these five usually provide a good starting point.

Work Breakdown Structure

What we have been doing over the past couple of topics is to identify the project deliverables and the work we will have to carry out to produce them. Then structuring the deliverables and work into project stages. We can now turn these stages, deliverables and tasks into what is called a Work Breakdown Structure (WBS).

Creating the WBS

We create a WBS by working top-down from the project itself and decompose the project into the project stages:

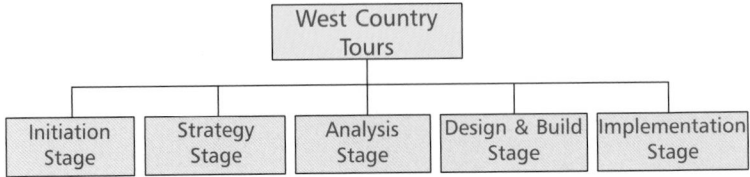

Then we can decompose each of the project stages into the deliverables that will be produced. In the following example we have decomposed the Analysis Stage into its deliverables:

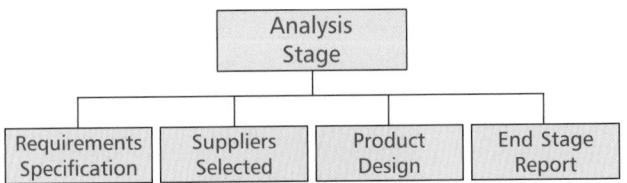

Then we can decompose each deliverable into the work tasks that will need to be carried out to produce it:

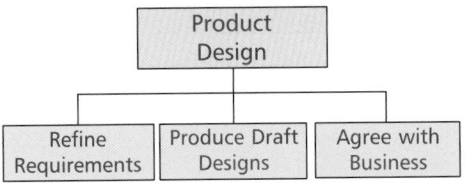

If necessary we can continue the process by decomposing each work task into sub-tasks or activities. There is an example of a partially completed WBS diagram opposite.

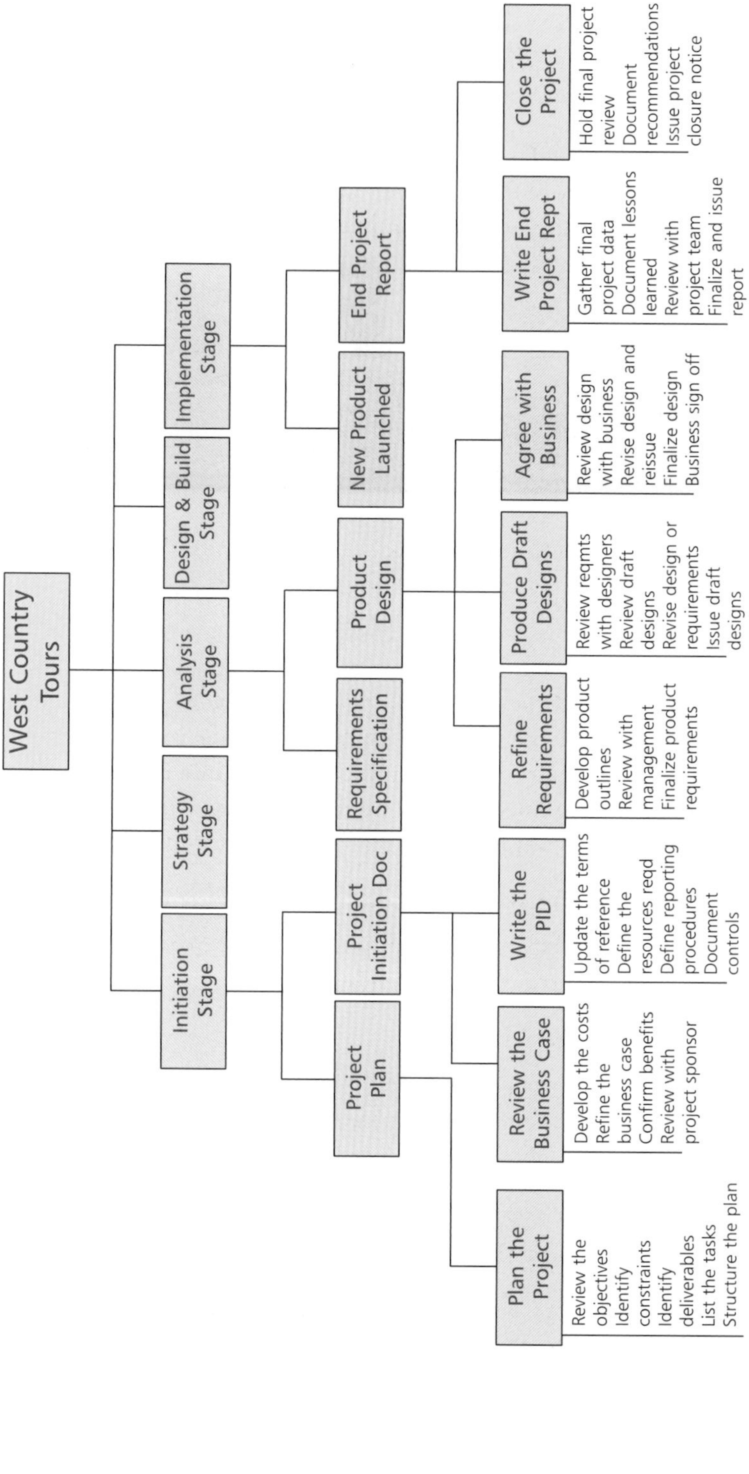

West Country Tours

- Initiation Stage
- Strategy Stage
- Analysis Stage
- Design & Build Stage
- Implementation Stage

Initiation Stage
- Project Plan
- Project Initiation Doc

Analysis Stage
- Requirements Specification
- Product Design

Implementation Stage
- New Product Launched
- End Project Report

Project Plan — Plan the Project
- Review the objectives
- Identify constraints
- Identify deliverables
- List the tasks
- Structure the plan

Review the Business Case
- Develop the costs
- Refine the business case
- Confirm benefits
- Review with project sponsor

Write the PID
- Update the terms of reference
- Define the resources reqd
- Define reporting procedures
- Document controls

Requirements Specification — Refine Requirements
- Develop product outlines
- Review with management
- Finalize product requirements

Product Design — Produce Draft Designs
- Review reqmts with designers
- Review draft designs
- Revise design or requirements
- Issue draft designs

Agree with Business
- Review design with business
- Revise design and reissue
- Finalize design
- Business sign off

End Project Report — Write End Project Rept
- Gather final project data
- Document lessons learned
- Review with project team
- Finalize and issue report

Close the Project
- Hold final project review
- Document recommendations
- Issue project closure notice

Beware

Several deliverables and tasks have been left out of this WBS in order to aid clarity.

Hot tip

When you run out of space across the page, list the next level below the task, as illustrated.

63

Estimating

Once a plan is produced (whether it's an initial, strategic, project plan or a detailed stage plan) the next step is to work out how long it will take to carry out. This is actually two steps, the first to estimate how much work is involved (the work effort) and the second to schedule how long that work will take (the duration). Once we have that information, we can also calculate how much it is going to cost.

The Real Cost of Projects

Contrary to popular belief, the main cost of new business systems is not normally the cost of the computer software or hardware. The main cost of implementing any form of new business system (computer or otherwise) is likely to be the time required (by the business) to implement it. This includes the time required by the project team to carry out the project and the time required by the end users to be trained on, and become familiar with, the new system. The estimating process fulfils two important purposes:

- It provides the basic 'manpower' time requirement to allow the project to be scheduled

- It allows the calculation of the true cost to the business of implementing a project

This information is fed back into the business case as the project duration and cost. These two factors enable the business to make a business decision about the project.

All Estimates are Wrong

When estimates are made the facts are not all known. Most of the facts will only become apparent later during the detailed work of the project, long after the initial estimate was produced. We shall see how to allow for this factor shortly.

One reason for breaking the project down into tasks is because that is the level that we need to estimate at, and even though all estimates are wrong, we still need to produce estimates which are as accurate as we can make them. So let's look at that process.

The Estimating Process

The best estimates are based on your own previous experience. If you have done something similar in the past you can use how long it took you last time.

If you haven't done anything similar in the past then try and find someone who has and ask them, that's the next best thing. If you can't find anyone to help, is there any published information on the subject? There is a wealth of information available in books, magazines and of course on the Internet.

Finally if all else fails take a guess. At the end of the day that's all you can do!

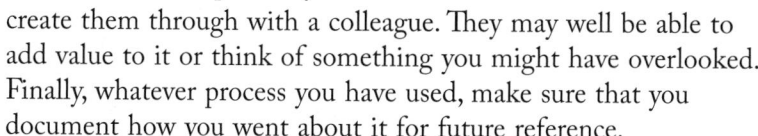

In estimating, as in a lot of other things, two heads are usually better than one, so talk your estimates and the process you have used to create them through with a colleague. They may well be able to add value to it or think of something you might have overlooked. Finally, whatever process you have used, make sure that you document how you went about it for future reference.

Re-estimating

Estimating and planning is not just a one-off process that we carry out at the start of a project, it is a reiterative process that goes on right through the project. We start off with a preliminary high-level estimate and plan in which there will be a lot of unknown factors. As we get further into a project and down into the detail, more information will come to light, so we need to keep on re-estimating and re-planning based on what we now know. This continues right up until we have completed the project.

If we keep re-estimating the chances are that our estimates will change as we do so (they should be getting more accurate). It is important to communicate this fact to your project sponsor so they know what is happening.

In the next topic we will look in a little more detail at the tasks and what size they should be.

 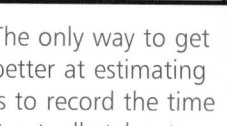

Task Size

In the previous topic we looked at the need to break work down into chunks, in order to be able to estimate it. But as well as being able to estimate how long chunks of work will take, the project manager also needs to control them and track their completion.

Progress Tracking

The problem is, people tend to be optimistic when they are asked when they can complete something by. That is no use when we are trying to measure progress. We need to use something reliable and we have already discussed what it is, the project deliverables.

Any chunk of work must have some sort of deliverable (output). If it's presenting a report to management, the deliverable is the final report, presented to management. So the only time we can know for certain that a chunk of work has been completed is when the deliverable has been produced (and if necessary accepted or approved by the business).

Hot tip

Tasks are the basic building blocks of a project. Through them you can estimate and control work.

Work Packets

To implement this, what we do is divide a project into chunks (or work packets) small enough for us to be able to estimate and schedule accurately. But these work packets must also be large enough to have deliverables, so that we can control them and identify when they have been completed.

So what is the largest chunk of work you would be comfortable with? Most people say somewhere between 3 and 10 days' work effort. Any more than ten and it becomes difficult to be accurate, unless it is simple, repetitive work. The ideal is around five days. One definition of a work packet that we have already used, and will use from now on, is a Task.

Tasks

We have defined our work packets as Tasks, these will typically require between 3 and 10 days' work effort (say 5 days on average) and must have at least one deliverable. A further aspect of tasks is that they don't exist in isolation. They will have inputs and dependencies, which means they will need something else to happen before they can begin and they will have other tasks dependent on them, which therefore cannot start until this particular task has been completed.

How Many Tasks?

At the start of a project there is no way of knowing how many tasks there are going to be in the project, let alone what they will be and how long they will take. But as a rough guide (based on experience) there are around 60 tasks in a typical small to medium sized project.

Beware

There is of course no such thing as a typical project!

If we use the typical task sizes we have just defined, that gives us a range of between 180 and 600 days' work effort for a typical project (around 300 days on average). You could now start to estimate the size of your project based on this alone, but there is one other point to make.

Project Estimate

Having previously divided the project into stages, and listed the deliverables and tasks required to produce them, we can now produce an initial estimate of the required work effort using the following steps:

1. Decide on the average task size (3 to 10 days, according to the size of the project), if you are not sure use 5 days as a default

2. Count up the number of tasks in each stage and multiply by the average task size, or substitute a different estimate if you have a clear idea of the amount of work effort in any specific task

3. Sum up the total days for each stage and decide if any stage looks too big or too small on this basis. If it does move some days between stages, add the stages up and that's your project work effort estimate

Beware

This is only a preliminary project estimate but it's better than nothing.

Summary

- Before starting to plan the project make sure you have established the business objectives and that they are SMART: Strategic, Measurable, Agreed, Realistic and Timed

- Once you have the objectives clearly stated you will need to find out what constraints the business will place on the project. These constraints will typically be of time, budget, availability of human and other resources, restrictions to the product you are producing and the organization's or other standards and regulations

- Start work on the plan by defining the ultimate deliverables, the things that the project must produce. Then work backwards through the project identifying what else will have to be produced along the way

- When you have identified the deliverables, you can then work out what tasks will need to be carried out to produce them

- Structure your plan by dividing the project into stages. The standard ones we use are: Initiation, Strategy, Analysis, Design & Build and Implementation, but these can be changed to suit the project and the organization

- Develop the structure of the project further by producing a Work Breakdown Structure, which decomposes the stages into deliverables and the deliverables into tasks

- Once we have decomposed the project down to the task level we can begin to estimate how much work effort there will be involved in carrying out each task and how long it will take to actually do it

- The best way to estimate a task is to base it on something similar you have done in the past, but if you haven't done anything similar, then ask other people, use published information if you can find it, but if all else fails take a guess

- The initial estimates we produce will be wrong as we do not really have enough information, later estimates will be more accurate

- Tasks should typically be between 3 and 10 days' work effort, say 5 days on average

5 Scheduling

Scheduling leads on from planning. It involves taking the planned work and predicting exactly when it needs to be carried out.

Work Effort & Duration

When we introduced the topic of estimating in the previous chapter, we mentioned work effort and duration. Although they are important for estimating, they are even more critical for scheduling, so it's worth making sure you have a clear idea of the difference. Assuming they are the same is a frequent cause of projects running late.

Work Effort

Our initial estimates should focus on the amount of work effort required to complete a piece of work. This is the time it should take one person working exclusively on this piece of work to complete it. It is usually expressed as people/days based on a standard working day or hours for a smaller task. For example, if based on experience we know that a piece of work will require ten solid days' work to complete it, this is the work effort.

If the work involved one person and the task was something like painting a warehouse, we might know from past experience it was going to require ten days' work effort. So if the person allocated to the task was going to work continuously on it and nothing else, then they might well be able to complete it in exactly ten working-days' duration.

Don't forget

Work Effort is the total amount of work that has to be done to complete a task. It is usually expressed in days or hours continuous work.

70

But in life generally and project work in particular, things are rarely that simple and straightforward. People will often have other things to do, so won't be available full-time. So we need to consider duration as something in its own right.

Duration

Once we have estimated the work effort we need to turn it into the duration, which is how long it will actually take to complete it. This needs to be based on calendar days.

If the task is to be completed by someone who is not available full-time and has other work tasks to complete then it will clearly take longer. Taking the painting example opposite, we may decide that we can allocate two people to work on it full-time, so the duration should come down to around five working days. But be warned as things are not normally as clear cut as that.

Non-working Time

In addition to allowing for any other work a person has to do, we also have to allow for non-work related activities that may happen in the same time frame. Might the person take a vacation? Is there a public holiday in their location? Might they be off work with an illness?

In addition to the types of non-working time we identified above, project team members often work for other parts of an organization and have things like department meetings to attend. We will look at how we can make allowances for all these factors in our schedules later in the chapter.

Beware

Never assume that work effort and duration are the same, they very rarely are.

71

Contingency

At the very start of a project we will know a lot less about it than we will by the time we are halfway through. Because of this we tend to underestimate the work involved in our early estimates. To compensate for this we need to increase our estimates and this is referred to as adding contingency.

How Much Contingency?

Clearly we will need to include a higher contingency figure at the start of the project, when we know least about it. Then as time goes by and we get further into the project we can reduce the amount we are adding as we will now know more. The following steps give a good rule of thumb for adding contingency:

1 Add 100% contingency at the start of the project. That's right, double the number you first thought of when you produce your first estimate

2 Reduce the contingency on the remainder of the project to 50% once you've determined the strategic requirements as you will now know quite a bit more about what the project is going to involve

3 Reduce the contingency to 25% on the remainder of the project when you've completed the analysis as you have now documented what will have to be done to meet the requirements

4 Finally reduce the contingency to 10% on the remainder of the project (the Implementation Stage) after you have completed the design and build

By reducing the contingency at each stage we are compensating for the things we now know that we didn't know before. The chances are that you will have used the contingency you had on the earlier work. If not, you didn't need it and you are a hero!

This may seem like a lot to add for the unknown, but experience has shown that these figures are not far out. There may be resistance to the use of such high figures, particularly on larger projects. However, experience again suggests, that the larger a project, the more likely it is to exceed initial estimates.

Hot tip

Smaller projects may not require as much contingency as these figures.

Hot tip

Be prepared to stand your ground on contingency, you will need it.

Profiling Contingency

There is one further complication that needs to be considered in applying contingency. The additional work that we are budgeting for needs to be profiled, that is it will not necessarily be spread evenly across the remainder of the project. It needs to be profiled so that the contingency is added where it is most likely to be needed. The following diagram illustrates how much we know about our project (our level of confidence) over time, starting from today.

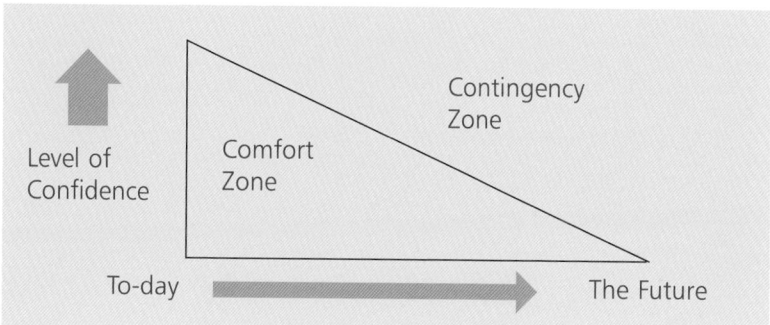

We usually know and can be confident about what we are going to be doing for the next couple of days. We also have a fairly good idea of what we will be doing on a project for the next week or two. But as we move further out into the future we have much less idea of what will be involved in say three or six months from now.

Back Loading

The implication of this is that we need to add less of contingency to the near future (the next stage) and more of it to the later stages. This is referred to as back loading.

But things are rarely straight forward in projects and you may actually know more about the final stage of the project than the middle. You may be able to profile the contingency on your project in a more sophisticated way, but if not, the above is usually a good general rule of thumb to apply.

We will look at how much contingency we should allow and how we should go about applying contingency to the estimate in the next topic.

Applying Contingency

As we saw in the previous topic, if a project is just starting, we need to add something in the region of 100% contingency to allow for all the unknown factors. As the project becomes further advanced, then we can reduce the contingency to say 50%, then 25% and finally 10% as appropriate. But these figures are just guidelines, if your project is larger or smaller you may want to increase or decrease the amount of contingency.

We also saw that the contingency needs to be profiled, with more contingency added the further in the future we are estimating. So let's take a look at applying contingency to an initial project estimate using the following steps:

1 Draw up a table (such as the one shown on the page opposite) with a row for each project stage plus a header and total row and six columns

2 For each stage of the project fill in the number of the stage, the number of deliverables and the number of tasks required to produce them

3 Decide on the average task size, for the example opposite we have assumed a small to medium project with an average task size of three days

4 Then multiply the number of tasks by the average task size and enter it in the days column for each stage

5 Total the number of days for the project and multiply it by your contingency factor, in the example opposite 100%

6 Apportion the contingency days from the last stage (highest contingency) back to the first stage (lowest contingency) and check that the contingency column adds up to the correct total

7 Add the contingency to the days for each stage to give you the total days and the total column then gives you the total for the project including contingency

Don't forget

There will be more uncertainty the further in the future something is going to happen.

Applying Contingency

The following table illustrates an example of the steps opposite. It represents a project with an average task size of three days.

Stage	Deliverable	Tasks	Days	Contingency	Total
1	2	2	6	1	7
2	2	3	9	3	12
3	3	4	12	6	18
4	10	12	36	38	74
5	5	7	21	36	57
Total	22	28	84	84	168

Using Contingency

The table above now includes 100% contingency to allow for the unknown factors at the start of the project. At the end of stage one you will have finished planning the project and produced the project initiation document. You now know more about the project and have probably identified more deliverables and tasks. So now we can revise the table:

1. Put the actual number of days spent for stage 1 in the days column, with zero contingency (the stage is finished so we no longer need contingency)

2. Now fill in the new estimate for the number of deliverables, tasks and the resultant days for the remaining stages

3. Now apply the new contingency figure, say 80% working back from the final stage in a similar way to the initial exercise

The results of the exercise should mean that the total for the project is close to the original estimate. As we get further into a project, and more facts become known, we should be able to produce better estimates for the remaining work and adjust (reduce) the amount of contingency to compensate for it.

Hot tip

Using contingency to keep your estimates and schedules consistent means you don't have to keep reporting changes to the business.

Scheduling

Scheduling involves taking the planned work effort estimates and translating them into elapsed, calendar time. In other words, showing when each Stage, Task and Activity will actually be started, how long they will take to carry out and when they will be completed. The schedule needs to be developed to the same level of detail as the project plan and estimate.

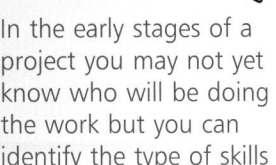

Hot tip

In the early stages of a project you may not yet know who will be doing the work but you can identify the type of skills they will need.

Allocating Work

Once we have an estimate for the work effort (the amount of work involved) in days or hours for any particular Task, we need to decide who is going to do it. Then we can allocate (assign) it to them and schedule it.

Scheduling Work

If someone was asked to carry out 45 days' work effort, and was relieved of all other work, how long should it take to complete it, in elapsed time? The first answer is often 'one and a half months' and that is the wrong answer. The second answer is often '9 weeks' which is better, but still wrong. To get the correct answer we need to consider unproductive time.

Unproductive Time

This is the time when people are on vacation, training, off sick, attending company meetings, etc. It also includes less well defined times when they are unproductive or having 'one of those days'.

If the project manager is in control of the project and has good communications within the team, they will know about most of the unproductive time. They should be able to schedule activities accurately for the next week or so. But that is unlikely to apply further ahead, say for the next three to nine months. So, for longer-term scheduling, we need a technique that takes all these factors into account. Let's look first at productive time.

Productive Time

There are of course 52 weeks in a year, but they are not all productive. So let's get rid of those unproductive weeks:

Hot tip

You may not agree with the detail of this model but it has been proven in practice, so try it out first and then adjust it as you like.

```
  52 calendar weeks in a year
- 4 weeks' vacation
- 2 weeks' public holidays
- 2 weeks' sickness
- 2 weeks' training
- 2 weeks for other things (development/self study)
  40 weeks
```

It leaves just 40 weeks and, for each of these weeks, there will be other factors that will impact on productivity. On average a person has half a day nonproductive each week (company meetings, filling in time sheets, making the coffee, talking to their friends, etc.). So, what we will actually get is 4.5 days' productive effort from them, for each of the 40 productive weeks.

That means we can schedule for 180 days work effort to be produced, by each full-time team member, in a calendar year. That's 15 days' work effort per month, so the correct answer to the question opposite is 3 months. But that's not quite the end of the story.

Hot tip

Make sure you really understand this basic scheduling guide as it has proved valid over many years.

Full or Part Time

Most project teams have members (often including the project manager) who are not full-time on the project. They have other work to do (their day jobs). If a person is allocated for 50% of their time to a project, they will produce 90 days' work effort in a year, at best. In practice, if someone only has half of his or her time allocated to a project, the project half will always suffer if there are issues in the day job. It is better to have 100% of someone's time allocated to the project for 3 months, than 50% of their time allocated to the project for 6 months.

Beware

If you don't take all these factors into account your schedules will fail.

Project Schedule

The first project schedule is normally produced during the project initiation stage. At that time not much detailed information is available, as the project is only just beginning, and consequently there will be a large amount of contingency to allow for the unknown factors. Therefore all it is practical to schedule is the strategic view showing the project stages. These should have been identified in the project plan and their work effort (including contingency) estimated.

The Gantt Chart

The high-level project schedule is best produced by mapping out each stage onto what is called a Gantt chart (named after Henry Gantt, a mechanical engineer, who developed the technique around 1915). They are one of the most useful tools in project management.

There are some useful tools for producing these charts (which we will look at in a later topic) but they can also be drawn up by hand (using squared paper) and they look like the following:

Project Stage	Jan	Feb	Mar	Apr	May	Jun	Jul	Aug	Sep
Initiation	▓								
Strategy		▓							
Analysis				▓					
Design & Build					▓	▓	▓		
Implementation								▓	

The way to develop the schedule as a Gantt chart is to carry out the following steps for each stage:

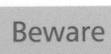 **1** Identify the number of people who are likely to be working on the stage and the percentage of their time that will be available, this will give you the number of full-time equivalent (FTE) people (say one person full time and two people at 50% gives us 2 FTE people)

 2 Take the work effort estimate for the stage (say 30 days) and divide it by the number of full-time equivalent people you have working on it (30 divided by 2 gives us 15 days)

Beware

The more people you add to a project, the more the project management overhead increases.

3   Using the scheduling guidelines we identified in the previous topic, we know that 15 days' work effort will take one elapsed month to complete, so we draw in a bar on the right-hand side of the chart one month long alongside this stage

4   Repeat the above steps for each further stage, starting to draw the next bar on the line below where the previous bar has stopped

When scheduling at this level, it is wise not to overlap stages, so work on the next stage should not begin until the previous stage has been completed. We will see why later and also see when there are exceptions, but for now accept it as 'good practice'.

What we have done so far is base our schedule on people's availability and ability to do work, but there are a number of further factors we need to consider when scheduling, even at the strategic level.

Approval Time

A common mistake in scheduling, is to forget the time it takes to get from the first draft of a document to the final approved version. If it is a critical document that has to go to senior management for approval (not unusual in project management), we need built in enough elapsed time for the production and approval of the final version of any key deliverables.

There will often be a key deliverable at the end of each stage. If these documents or products have to go to senior management for approval it might be wise to allow a gap of say one week between the end of one stage and the start of the next stage.

Reality Check

When you complete the schedule for your project for the first time you will have the answer to the key question: How long will it take? This almost certainly is going to be longer than the business wanted or expected. You may have pressure put on you to reduce the overall time but be careful, if you start reducing the elapsed time for the project you will be increasing the risks.

Hot tip

We will look at how to deal with this situation and risk management in later topics.

Network Diagrams

The fundamental idea behind network diagrams is to represent graphically the sequential relationship between the tasks in a project. The diagrams can be developed initially without knowing how long the tasks will take or when they will actually be performed, although this information can later be added. The diagram itself doesn't change (unlike a Gantt chart).

There are several variations of network techniques but the two most commonly used in project management are: Activity on arrow and Activity on node. We will look at both, starting with an activity on arrow network diagram:

Activity on Arrow

The following diagram illustrates one section of a simple activity on arrow network diagram:

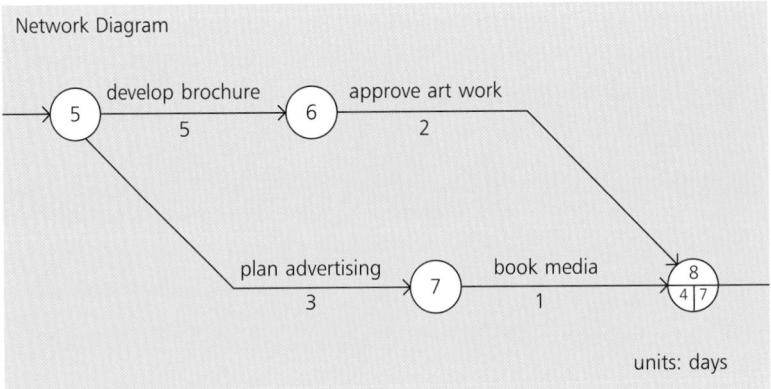

In this diagram the arrows represent the project tasks, with the task name shown above the line. Once the duration (not the work effort) is known it can be added and is shown beneath the line. The duration is normally shown as a whole number of days or hours and, in order not to clutter the diagram up the units are shown in the bottom right-hand corner of the diagram.

The circles are called Nodes and they represent events, points in time of zero duration (effectively very small milestones). The node numbers: 5, 6, 7 and 8 are just references. The nodes can also be enhanced to show the earliest and latest event time as a day number (from zero at the start of the project or diagram) as illustrated above for node 8. This type of diagram is useful where there are a lot of complex inter-relationships.

Activity on Node

The other most commonly used type of network diagram is the activity on node diagram. This is effectively the opposite of the activity on arrow diagram as, in this case, the nodes represent the tasks and the arrows the links between them. Each node consists of a number of segments which are used to hold different bits of information, as illustrated:

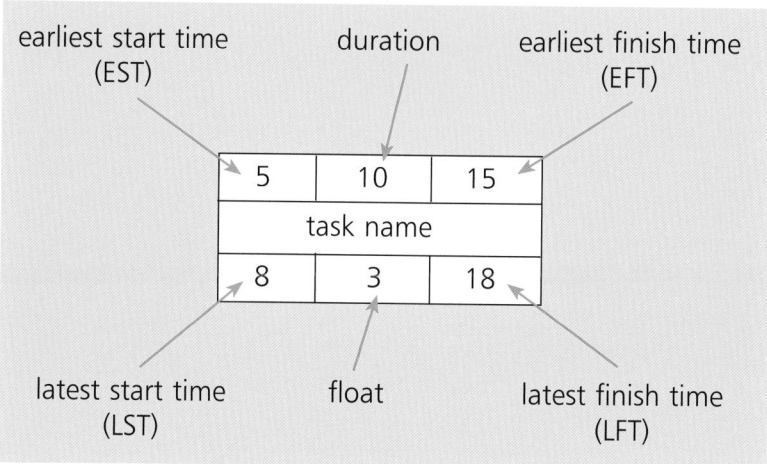

The numbers are all in days and the earliest start time is counted as the number of days from the start of the project and the earliest finish time is the EST plus the duration. The latest start time is again counting from the start of the project and the latest finish time is the LST plus the duration. The float is the difference between the earliest and latest times and represents the number of days the task can 'float' backwards or forwards without impacting the project. The following illustrates a small diagram:

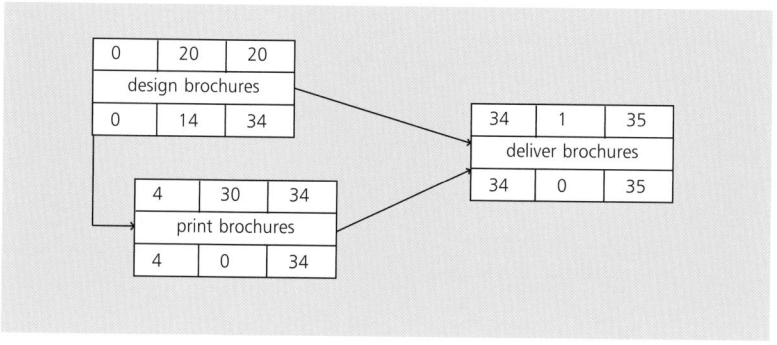

Gantt Charts

We have already illustrated a couple of simple Gantt charts but just to recap, let's look at the last one again:

Project Stage	Jan	Feb	Mar	Apr	May	Jun	Jul	Aug	Sep
Initiation	██								
Strategy		███	██						
Analysis				██					
Design & Build					███	███	███		
Implementation								███	██

The left-hand side of the chart is where we list the activities, in this case it is the project stages. The right-hand side is where we draw bars to represent the duration of each activity. The bit across the top is the time scale, in this case months. But this is a very simple and high-level Gantt chart. We can put a lot more detail into Gantt charts and a slightly more complex and detailed Gantt chart is illustrated opposite.

Gantt Detail

In the Gantt chart opposite we are now showing two levels from our work breakdown structure: Stages and Tasks. The stage names are highlighted in bold and the summary bars on the chart showing duration are in black.

Beneath each stage name we have listed the tasks in the stage and inserted two new columns, one for the duration (Dur) and one for the start date (Start). The bars showing the task durations are in blue.

We have also 'zoomed in' on the time scale and are showing one box for each day. The weekends are greyed out as non-working days and they are not counted as part of the duration (which is stated in working days).

Even More Detail

Although we have added more detail compared to the simple Gantt chart above, there is still a lot more detail we could add. It would be useful to have the end dates, who was allocated to work on each task and link lines between tasks (as in network diagrams). To add this level of detail we would need some form of planning tool and we will be looking at one in the next topic.

Task Name	Dur	Start
Initiation Stage		
Plan the project	2	Jan 02
Review business case	1	Jan 04
Identify resources	1	Jan 05
Obtain agreement	3	Jan 08
Schedule kick off	1	Jan 12
Produce draft PID	3	Jan 17
Review with sponsor	1	Jan 21
Kick off meeting	1	Jan 26
End stage report	2	Jan 30
Strategy Stage		
Schedule interviews	1	Feb 05
Carry out interviews	10	Feb 12
Draft report	5	Feb 26
Present findings	1	Mar 05
Finalize report	2	Mar 06
Business sign off	5	Mar 13
End stage report	2	Mar 14
Analysis Stage		

Scheduling Tools

There are a number of project planning and scheduling tools available of which Microsoft Project is by far the most popular. These tool will provide a range of different features and functionality but they all consist of a set of basic functions for creating and maintaining a Gantt chart. The following illustrates a Gantt chart as created in Microsoft Project:

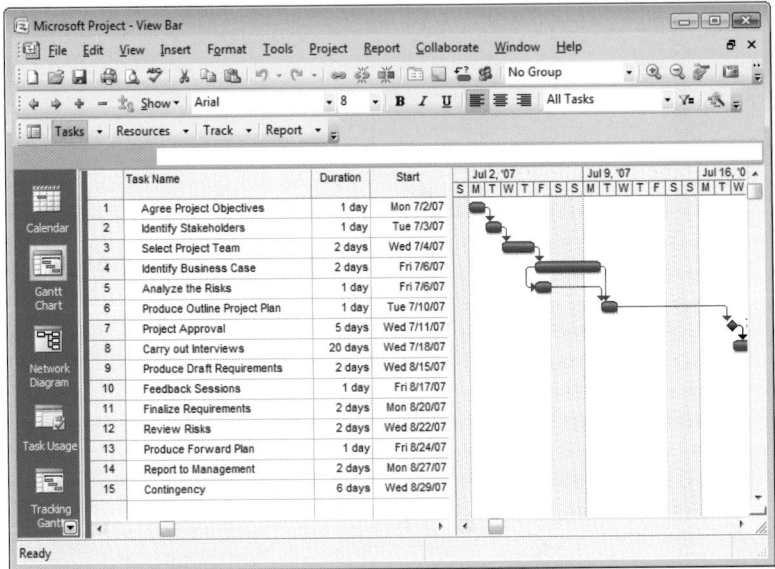

These tools give us the same basic information as we had on our hand drawn charts. But they hold a lot of additional information on tasks (end dates, task dependencies and resources allocated). They can also hold a lot of information on resources:

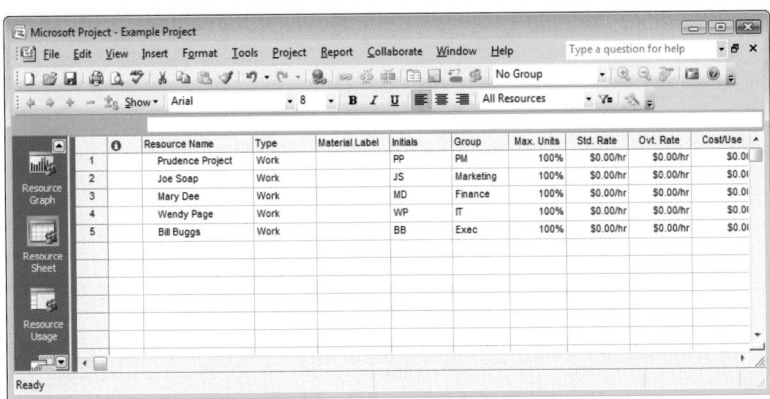

Project planning and scheduling tools give you a number of useful features such as:

- They provide wizards and other help features to guide you through the process of creating your plan and schedule

- Once created they can help you update and manage your schedule and track progress against it

- They can produce a critical path analysis to identify areas where you need to keep a close track on progress

- They can identify if you have too much work allocated to anyone and can level work (by spreading it backwards or forwards) manually or automatically

- They can schedule materials and facilities as well as human resources

- They can track costs against a project budget

- They keep track of public holidays and people's vacations

- They can help you develop professional looking reports and present information in an effective and understandable way

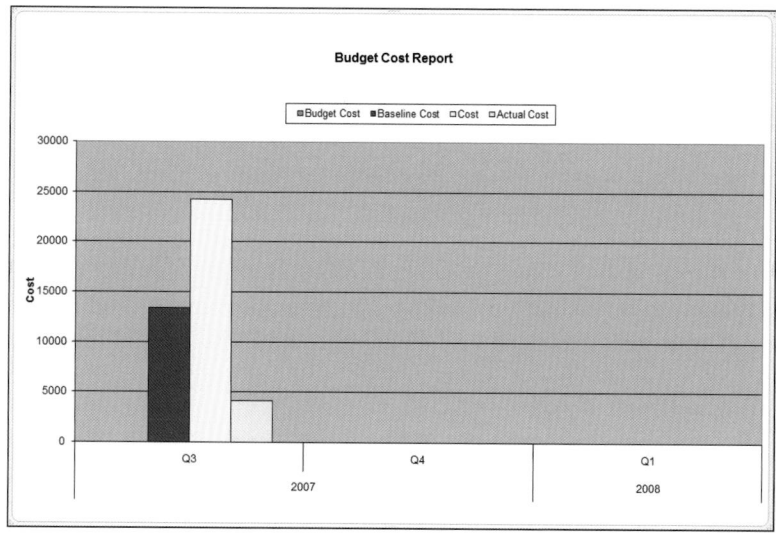

The above illustration shows an example of the type of chart that can be used to report on progress.

Critical Path

The critical path is the term given to the sequence of tasks that are critical to the duration of the project. A critical task is one that, if delayed or lengthened, will directly affect the project finish date.

The following diagram represents a simple project consisting of just four tasks. Tasks A, B and D are each of two days' duration, while Task C is of one day's duration. Tasks B and C are both dependent on Task A (that is they cannot be started until Task A has been completed). Likewise Task D is dependent on both Tasks B and C being completed before it can start.

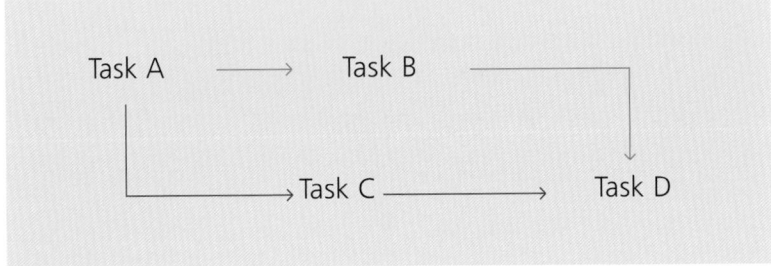

As Tasks B and C can take place at the same time the overall duration of the project is six days.

Non-critical Tasks
Even if Task C were to slip by one day it would not impact the completion of Task D, as that task has to wait for the completion of Task B as well, so it would not impact the completion of the project. Task C is therefore deemed to be a non-critical task.

Critical Tasks
On the other had if any of Tasks A, B or D were to slip by one day the project would now take seven days to complete and not six. Therefore Tasks A, B and D are deemed to be critical tasks.

The Critical Path
The critical path is therefore the path (or paths) through the project that link critical tasks. In the diagram above it is shown in red while the non-critical path is shown in blue.

In network diagrams (which are typically produced in black and white) the critical path is shown as a double width line or heavy black line.

Developing the Schedule

As well as producing the project level plan and schedule, we need to produce more detailed stage plans and schedules.

Stage Plans & Schedules

In fact, the very first plan and schedule to be produced is the Initiation Stage Plan, which should be produced during start up. This is before the first full project plan (which is produced during the Initiation Stage). Back in Chapter 2 we covered the Initiation Stage Plan, but we have now gone into a lot more detail about planning, estimating and scheduling, so it might be worth taking another look at it now, to see if there is anything that should be changed.

The next stage plan and schedule will be produced towards the end of the Initiation Stage and is covered later.

Updating your Plan and Schedule

Once we've produced the project plan, estimate and schedule; we need to verify that it will work. In fact, it might even be wise to assume that we have made mistakes and missed things in our early plans. The best way of finding out, is to go through the plan, estimate and schedule with the other people in the project team. Explain it to them, and get them to look at and understand it. Just doing this is often enough to reveal the faults. The more often it's done, the better the plan gets. It will also help to get their buy in and commitment and build team ownership of the plan and schedule, after all they are the people who are going to be doing it.

Baseline

The plan and schedule will need to be reviewed and revised in the light of what actually happens in practice (it's never quite the same as the plan). It will need to be revised if a requirement (or anything else) changes, particularly if it will affect a deliverable.

But it is also important that we don't lose sight of the original plan, when making these changes. The best way of achieving this is to freeze the original plan, once it has been approved. This is called setting a 'baseline'. Then, changes are always reflected against and compared to the original baseline.

This way we can see how much things have changed and prevent scope creep (always a risk when revising plans).

Summary

- Work effort is the total amount of work that has to be performed to complete a task and the duration is the elapsed amount of time it will take to complete it. They are rarely the same thing

- You need to add contingency to your project to allow for the things that you don't know about when producing your early estimates

- Contingency should be profiled as you will usually require more contingency the further in the future something will be happening

- When scheduling use 180 productive days per full-time person/year to allow for non-productive and non-working time

- Gantt charts provide a very useful high-level view of the project and can easily be drawn on squared paper

- When producing your schedules remember to allow time for approval of key documents or other deliverables

- Network diagrams are useful if you have a lot of task inter-relationships and you can choose between activity on arrow or activity on node

- Detailed Gantt charts at the task level are normally drawn at the days within weeks level so that you can see exactly when a task is due to start and end

- Planning and scheduling tools, such as Microsoft Project, are useful for producing and maintaining Gantt charts and network diagrams but they can do a lot more besides

- The critical path is the path through a Gantt chart or network diagram that highlights the tasks that will delay the project end date if they slip

- As well as producing the project plan and schedule, we also need to produce more detailed stage plans and schedules

- Once the project plan is agreed it should be saved and 'baselined' for comparison with later versions

6 Risk Management

Failure to manage risks is a common cause of project failure. This chapter deals with their identification, evaluation and the development of any required countermeasures.

Types of Risk

The management of risk involves more than just identifying and dealing with risks to the project. It also involves being aware of, and dealing with, risks to the business. Risks that the project itself may well create. So let's look at the two types of risk:

Business Risks

Even though a project may be completed on time and to budget (which has traditionally been the definition of a successful project) it may still not result in the delivery of the benefits envisaged by the business case. While it is the project sponsor (or steering committee) who should identify and manage them, business risks must still be recognized. These are some of the risks that might be relevant:

Viability of the Business Case

While some business cases may show a substantial benefit for a relatively low cost, in others the balance between costs and benefits may be quite narrow. There may be other factors that could change the balance or it may be that when more information becomes available, it changes the costs or benefits. These types of factors can impact on the basic viability of the business case and are potential business risks.

Market Changes

The market in which the business operates may change as a result of new products or services becoming available. Exchange rates can fluctuate and the economic climate itself can change. Any of these things could make the results of the project less viable.

Legislative Changes

In addition to market change, changes in the law requiring a different way of working or new information to be maintained can have a profound impact on the viability of a project. These need to be recognized and their impact on the business case considered as they could make the results of the project useless.

These are all typical business risks associated with projects.

Project Risks

On the other hand project risks represent threats to the project itself and therefore to the achievement of the project's objectives within budget and on time. The typical types of risks under this heading are things like:

Beware

The project will not be a success, even if it is completed on time and to budget, if there is no benefit to the business.

Supplier Failure

A project will often be dependent on one or more external (or internal) suppliers for the delivery of key parts of the project. These suppliers could be late with their delivery, they could fail to meet the business requirements or they could even go out of business. Any of these factors could have a serious impact on a project and they are not uncommon.

Skill Shortage

During the planning and scheduling of the project, certain assumptions will have been made about the availability of key people or key skills. In practice, key people are sometimes not available. They may be needed for other more strategic activities within the business or they could choose to leave for another job. These things (which have a tendency to happen at the worst possible time) could have a serious impact on the project.

New Methods

Due to the unique nature of projects, people will often be doing unfamiliar tasks and activities. This can result in things taking longer than expected (because of the learning curve) or in mistakes being made (with the need for work to be corrected or redone). Any of these factors will all have an impact on the project.

The underlying message is proceed with caution, there could be risks from contractual problems, culture clashes between stakeholders and potential risks from any specialist or technical areas involved.

Don't forget

These are only some examples of risks, your project will be different.

Managing Risk

Managing Risk is one of the key responsibilities of the project manager and project sponsor (or steering committee). The project manager is responsible for actually managing the risks and the project sponsor for keeping the project manager informed of external risks and making decisions based on the project manager's recommendations.

The actual process of managing risk splits into two phases: Risk Analysis (when the risks are first identified) and Risk Management (the ongoing actions taken to deal with them). Running alongside this will be the ongoing recording and updating of the risks in a Risk Log.

Risk Analysis

Risk Analysis involves identifying risks, estimation of their potential impact and evaluating what should be done about them. It consists of three steps:

1 Risk Identification to recognize and determine the potential risks

2 Risk Estimation to determine how important or critical each risk is

3 Risk Evaluation to decide what countermeasures should be taken to deal with each risk

Hot tip

Risk Management continues for the life of the project.

Risk Log

The Risk Log is a continuously updated record of all identified risks, with what has or is being done about each of them and their current status. The criticality of risks can vary and what may be a minor risk one day may be a far more significant risk on another.

Risk Management

Risk Management then involves the actual actions required to deal with and control the risks. It consists of four steps:

1. Planning to identify what needs to be done to deal with a risk and how we will do it

2. Resourcing to calculate what additional resources we will need to do it

3. Monitoring to watch for signs of the risk happening, as a continual process

4. Controlling to ensure that what we have planned actually happens

The following topics work through each of the risk analysis activities, taking countermeasures, the risk log and the risk management process.

Risk Identification

The starting point for the whole process is identifying the potential risks to the project and the business.

Source of Risks

One of the sections of the Terms of Reference (which is prepared during project start up) is a list of any known risks (including both project and business risks). Additional risks may be identified through discussion with the project sponsor and other stakeholders.

Preparing the Project Initiation Document (during the Initiation Stage) will often bring additional risks to light. Developing the project plan and schedule will almost always bring other risks to mind. Project team meetings and formal reviews are also likely sources of risk identification.

It is worth while having a regular, scheduled risk review with the project team, as part of a project team meeting at least once a month. It is also a good opportunity to review and update the risk log at the same time.

Don't forget

Review your risks regularly.

In the early stages of the project, a brainstorming session on risks is an excellent way of getting things started. The ideal time to do it is at the project kick off meeting after going through the project plan with the team.

Risk Identification

To start the process of identifying your project risks carry out the following steps:

1 Look at the examples of risks listed at the start of this chapter and consider if any of them could apply to your project

2 List them on a sheet of paper, leaving some space on the right-hand side for later use

3 Now think about any other risks that could apply to your project and your business and add them all to your list

The example below lists the potential risks that could be identified for our example project, South West Tours.

Risk	Risk Description
001	Failure of a key supplier after bookings are taken
002	Failure to secure necessary holiday accommodation
003	Insufficient hire bikes available for holiday bookings
004	Brochures not ready on time for launch
005	Brochure quality not satisfactory
006	Planned staff levels unable to cope with workload
007	Loss of key project team member at a critical time
008	Failure of the business to secure sufficient holiday bookings

Giving risks a unique identification number will help to keep track of the risks. The final two columns on the right-hand side of the form will be completed in the next topic.

Risk Estimation

Clearly just identifying risks will not make them go away, something has to be done about them. But risks are not all equal, some could be quite trivial, while others could cause the project, or even the business, to fail. So it is important to identify which ones need to be addressed, by assessing their probability and impact.

Probability

We use probability to gauge how likely it is that the risk will happen?

The most straight forward approach is to rate the probability on a high/medium/low scale. High would suggest that the risk is probably going to happen (i.e. more likely to occur than not), medium would indicate a possible (50/50 chance) and low that the risk is unlikely to happen.

Impact

Once we have estimated the probability of the risk happening, we can go on to think about what impact it will have on the project (or business) if the risk does occur. Again the most straight forward approach is to use the same high/medium/low scale for the impact.

This time high means it would have a serious impact on the project or business (posing a serious threat), medium if it would have a medium impact (say causing a significant delay or a significant increase in cost) and low if it would not be that important (a minor annoyance or delay or a slight increase in cost).

Risk Estimation

Now look back at the list of risks you produced in the previous topic and carry out the following additional steps:

1 Label the two right-hand columns on your risk sheet "Probability" and "Impact"

2 Consider each risk in turn and rate its probability as High, Medium or Low

3 In the light of that now consider each risk and rate it for impact as High, Medium or Low

The following table is again based on our example project, South West Tours:

Risk	Risk Description	Probability	Impact
001	Failure of a key supplier after bookings are taken	Medium	High
002	Failure to secure necessary holiday accommodation	Medium	High
003	Insufficient hire bikes available for holiday bookings	Low	High
004	Brochures not ready on time for launch	Medium	High
005	Brochure quality not satisfactory	Medium	Medium
006	Planned staff levels unable to cope with workload	Medium	Medium
007	Loss of key project team member at a critical time	Low	High
008	Failure of the business to secure sufficient holiday bookings	Medium	Medium

If you have followed this and the previous topic you will have performed an initial risk identification and risk estimation exercise on your project. This method, using High, Medium and Low is a fairly simple and straight forward method of risk estimation. There are far more complex methods, typically using a scale of one to ten, but in practice this degree of complexity makes it far less obvious to see the underlying criticality. In this case Keeping It Simple and Straight forward (KISS) really does pay off.

Risk Evaluation

Having rated the probability and potential impact of the identified risks, a decision can be made on which ones need to be addressed. The following diagram is referred to as a Probability Impact Grid and it sets out the priorities quite clearly:

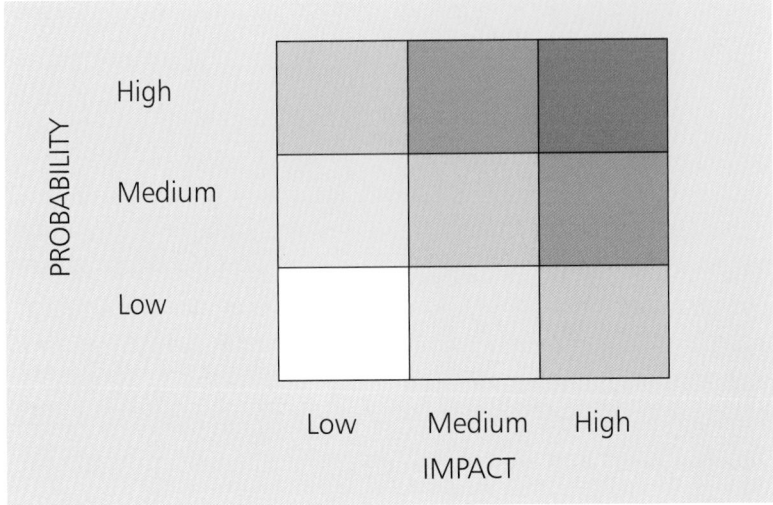

Beware

If you have identified a High Probability/High Impact risk it is critical to deal with it.

Priority Risks

Any risks which fall in the High Probability/High Impact area must be addressed as a top priority. These are risks which will probably happen and when they do they will have a significant impact on the project or the business. Clearly these risks need to have urgent attention.

Second Priority

Once the top priority risks have been addressed, we can turn our attention to the second priority risks, these are the High Probability/Medium Impact and Medium Probability/High Impact risks. These risks also need to be dealt with urgently as they too can seriously impact the project.

The chances are that high probability risks will occur and when they do, they will have an impact on the project, either in terms of delays or costs or possibly both. Medium probability risks have a 50/50 chance of occurring, which is still quite a high probability. If they do occur they will have a significant impact on the project in terms of serious delays or significant extra costs. Clearly both need to be addressed.

Medium Priority

Once the High/High and High/Medium risks have been addressed and only when they have been addressed, we can turn our attention to the third category of risks. These are the High/Low, Medium/Medium and Low/High risks. These can now be considered and a decision made on whether they can and should be addressed.

By now we can start making a value judgement. Does the cost of dealing with the risk outweigh the risk itself. We can now decide on taking possible low cost actions.

Low Priority

Finally, when we have dealt with the medium priority risks, all we have left is the Medium/Low, Low/Medium and Low/Low risks. These are normally just accepted as they are either not going to have a significant impact on the project or are very unlikely to occur, if not both.

Performing a Risk Evaluation

You can now go back to your initial list of risks developed in the previous two topics and carry out the following steps:

1.   Decide which risks must be dealt with as a top priority, these will be any High/High risks and any High/Medium or Medium/High risks which could significantly threaten the project or the business

2.   Work your way through the other High/Medium and Medium/High risks and confirm that they have been assessed correctly and if so prioritize them to be dealt with next

3.   Finally examine the other risks and make sure they have not been underestimated, these can be marked down for consideration once the high priority risks have been dealt with

Once you have decided on the prioritization of the risks, you can consider the appropriate types of countermeasure or actions that need to be taken. These are covered in the next topic.

Hot tip

Identify all your risks, estimate their probability and impact and then evaluate which ones you need to deal with.

Countermeasures

There are five main options for dealing with each project or business risk:

Prevention

This is appropriate where a risk must be prevented from happening, whatever the cost. Risk prevention will usually involve significant costs and they may be enough to nullify the benefits of the project. Opting for prevention is therefore usually a last resort.

Reduction

Where it is not appropriate or financially feasible to prevent a risk completely it may be possible to take steps to reduce the likelihood of the risk happening or perhaps to reduce the impact if it does occur. These steps may still involve costs but they are not usually as significant as for prevention.

Acceptance

Sometimes the risk just has to be accepted. This may be because the risk is considered insignificant or it may be that the cost of any countermeasure would be far too great. Whatever the reason, this option is effectively gambling on the risk not occurring or not impacting the project too significantly if it does occur.

Transfer

In theory it is possible to transfer a risk to someone else by taking out an insurance policy or asking a supplier to carry the risk. This is typically implemented by making the supplier responsible for any delays. But in reality the risk will still be there, what is being transferred is the implementation of the countermeasures and these will usually involve some cost. The supplier will need to build in some form of contingency or insurance against the risk occurring.

Contingency Plan

A contingency plan is some form of back up plan prepared in advance that will be brought into play if the risk occurs at a later date. Sometimes just the addition of contingency time to the schedule will be enough.

These countermeasures are not exclusive and sometimes more than one option may be appropriate. Often a combination of several options is the best approach. As you work through your project risks, consider each of these types of countermeasure.

Beware

Avoidance (wishing a risk will go away) is not an option!

Deciding on Countermeasures

You should now be able to go back to your list of risks from the previous topics and decide on the appropriate type of countermeasures for each. When you have done that you should make a note of the steps you are taking to implement the countermeasures.

The following table lists the countermeasures and notes for our example project, South West Tours. It is based on the risks and risk assessments in the previous two examples.

Risk	Countermeasure	Notes
001	Contingency Plan	Identify alternative suppliers
002	Prevent/Reduce	Locate accommodation early in the project and sign agreements with suppliers
002	Contingency Plan	Identify alternative accommodation suppliers
003	Prevent	Ensure lead time is established and plan on that basis
003	Transfer	Ask main business to accept risk and provide contingency plan
004	Reduce	Establish the critical nature of the venture with suppliers and monitor production closely
005	Prevent	Implement formal quality control procedures with supplier
006	Contingency	Plan for additional temporary staff if needed
007	Contingency	Prepare contingency plan for each key member of staff
008	Accept	Business risk - no impact on the project

If you have worked through the past three topics, you have now completed your Risk Analysis and it's time to create a Risk Log and enter the appropriate data. We will be looking at how to do that in the next topic.

Risk Log

It is sad to say but true, that if we don't record all our risks they will get forgotten. It is also extremely useful to have a record of how they were assessed, what countermeasures were taken, when and why. This is also important, as it is usual to review risks at certain set times during a project.

The record of risks is referred to as a Risk Log and its contents form a history of risks. Typically it will be a word-processed table or a spreadsheet with the following columns:

Risk ID
A unique identifier for the risk. Usually just a sequential number.

Risk Type
Whether the risk is a business risk, a project risk or both.

Author
The person who identified or documented the risk.

Date Identified
The date when the risk was first documented.

Last Updated
The date the risk was last changed.

Description
Narrative description of the nature of the risk.

Probability
High, Medium or Low.

Impact
High, Medium or Low.

Countermeasures
Planned or actually being taken.

Owner
The person responsible for taking the countermeasures.

Status
The current status of the risk.

Opposite there is an example of a complete risk log for South West Tours (some column headings have been abbreviated).

Risk ID	Risk Type	Aut	Date Identified	Last Updated	Description	Prob	Imp	Counter	Own	Status
001	Project	PP	04/05/10	04/06/10	Failure of key supplier	Med	High	Contingency	PP	Looking for alternatives
002	Project	PP	04/05/10	04/05/10	Failure to secure accommodation	Med	High	Reduce + Contingency	PP BB	Locate early + locate alternates
003	Project	PP	04/05/10	04/05/10	Insufficient bikes available	Low	High	Prevent + Transfer	PP	Lead time + transfer to business
004	Project	BB	04/05/10	04/05/10	Brochures late from printers	Med	High	Reduce	PP	Monitor progress closely
005	Project	BB	04/05/10	04/05/10	Brochure quality not satisfactory	Med	Med	Prevent	BB	Formal quality control
006	Project	FL	04/05/10	04/05/10	Planned staff levels unable to cope	Med	Med	Contingency	BB	Take on temps to cover launch period
007	Project	PP	04/05/10	04/05/10	Loss of team member at bad time	Low	High	Contingency	PP	Plan for each key team member
008	Business	PP	04/05/10	04/05/10	Failure to secure sufficient bookings	Med	Med	Accept	BB	Business risk only, accepted by business

Don't forget

It may be necessary to take more than one type of countermeasure.

103

Risk Management

Once the risks have been identified, assessed, evaluated and recorded in the risk log, risk management can begin. This involves four main activities:

Planning

For each identified countermeasure, the quantity and type of resources (people or otherwise) that will be required to carry out the necessary actions needs to be identified. Then the necessary tasks to carry them out need to be added to the appropriate stage plan. Finally, the desirability of carrying out the actions and the plan revisions need to be agreed and approved by the project sponsor or steering committee.

Resourcing

Once the countermeasures have been planned and agreed, the actual people (or other resources) that will be required to carry them out, need to be identified and allocated to the tasks. These will usually have additional costs which could take the project outside of its budget. If this is the case then the business case will need to be revised and the additional costs authorised.

Where the actions are contingency actions, decisions need to be made about how the contingency actions will be funded, if and when they become necessary.

Monitoring

Once the countermeasures are planned and resourced, the project needs to be monitored, on an ongoing basis, to ensure that any potential risks are spotted as soon as they occur. Then any necessary contingency plans can be brought into action to deal with the risks.

Controlling

Finally once countermeasures have been initiated, the necessary actions need to be controlled to make sure they happen as they are supposed to.

The management of risk should continue throughout the life of the project, with regular risk reviews being scheduled and held.

Planning, resourcing, monitoring and controlling are all developed further, later in the book.

Hot tip

Make sure you continue managing risks until they have been fully resolved.

Summary

- There are two types of risk: business risks (such as the viability of the business case, market changes and legislative changes) and project risks (such as supplier failure, skills shortages and new methods)

- The management of risk consists of risk analysis (identification, estimation and evaluation), risk recording and risk management (planning, resourcing, monitoring and controlling)

- Risks can be identified from a variety of sources: existing documentation, discussion with stakeholders, planning and project team meetings

- It is worth scheduling a regular risk review with your project team, say once a month

- Risk estimation consists of working out the probability (how likely the risk is to happen) and the impact (what it will do to the project or business if it does happen)

- Risk evaluation is the process of determining which risks you need to take steps to deal with and which you can accept

- Risk countermeasures consist of five options: prevention (always the most costly), reduction (of probability or impact), acceptance, transference and contingency planning

- All risks need to be captured in some form of Risk Log, this should record all the information about the risk, who it was raised by and when, who the countermeasures are allocated to and when the risk was last updated

- The risk log should form a growing record of what has been done with the risk from it being first identified until it can be closed

- Once a risk has been analyzed and recorded, risk management takes over. This is the ongoing process that consists of planning, resourcing, monitoring and controlling the risk until it can be closed

- The management of risks should start at the beginning and continue for the life of the project

7 Organizing

Organizing is all about getting down to the detail. This chapter looks at developing stage plans, activity schedules and documentation.

Getting Organized

This book deals with the four key skills needed by a project manager. The first was planning, which was covered in chapter four. Now we get down to the nitty-gritty, day to day skill of organizing the work of the project.

Organizing

Organizing is a key management skill and, if it is important for managers, it's doubly important for project managers. Would you trust someone who couldn't get themselves organized to manage a project?

Organized People

But what is the basic essence of organizing? Why can some people seem to do it naturally, while others struggle under a mountain of paper? Think about the organized people you know. What are the signs that tell you that they are organized?

The sorts of things we usually identify with organized people are:

- a tidy (but not necessarily empty!) desk

- everything is in its place

- they can always find the piece of paper, document or file they are looking for

- they can always get hold of any information they need as they know where to go for it

- they may not necessarily know all the answer themselves, but they do know where to go to get them

Structured Activities

The secret to successful organization is to structure your work or activities in some way. You should only have the details of your current task or tasks (but never too many at once) on your desk at any one time. Everything should be filed away in an organized manner until you need it.

Time Management

When time management was first the vogue, it was compulsory to go on a two-day time management course before you could have your 'prestigious' time management folder. Despite the fact that some people resented having to 'waste' two days' training, rather than getting on with (already late) projects, most found it beneficial. It turned out to be all about getting organized. It introduced a focus on a limited number of key activities. These were the strategic things that mattered in our jobs and in our lives. Most came away having learnt something useful, as well as clutching their new time management folders!

Project Structure

One of the reasons for structuring a project is that it's a good way of organizing work. We defined our top level structure as the five (or however many is appropriate) project stages. If you have been working through the steps in this book, you will have defined the key deliverables for your project under these stages. You will have already begun the process of organizing your project by producing the strategic project plan. The next step was to produce a more detailed plan for a single stage (a Stage Plan) by dividing the stage into its constituent Tasks. We can continue this process and divide the tasks down into their constituent activities.

Hot tip

It doesn't matter what system you use for getting organized, just find a way that works for you and use it.

109

Resources

During project start up and the initiation stage, the required skills should have been identified and suitable project team members recruited, either from within the organization or externally as appropriate. There are a number of steps that need to be taken to organize these resources in order to get the most effective use of their time:

Contact Details

The first priority is to gather the team's contact details. This will enable them to contact each other and start networking:

1 Produce a full list of the team members, with their location, the department or organization they work for, their postal address, e-mail address, and fixed and mobile telephone numbers

2 If it is a large or dispersed team consider the inclusion of their photographs, to aid recognition

3 Copy this information to all the team members so they can all contact each other direct

Team Meetings

Team meetings are critical to the success of a project and an excellent vehicle for organizing the work.

1 Organize a project kick off meeting as soon as possible and include the whole team

2 Hold regular team progress meetings, typically weekly or possibly monthly, depending on the needs of the project

3 Try to organize face to face meetings at key times during the project such as when a particularly difficult stage has been completed

Hot tip

The project kick-off meeting is a really great way of getting a team working together.

The kick off meeting is particularly important if it is a large and dispersed team. It may be the only time they ever meet in person as the subsequent meetings may need to be by video-conference or telephone conference call.

Skills Matrix

The next priority is to develop a skills matrix. You will know that a team member has been selected for the project because they possess a particular skill or ability, which the project needed. What you may not know is what other skills and abilities they have that might also be useful for the project.

1. Meet each team member, one to one, face to face and ask them about themselves, what they expect to get out of the project and what skills and abilities they have

2. Build up a skills matrix with the team members listed on one axis and the skills they possess on the other

This will be invaluable when you come to allocate and schedule the project tasks and activities. The other invaluable aid for this activity is an availability matrix.

Availability Matrix

Similar to the skills matrix but this one has the team members across the top and time down the left-hand side. If you need greater detail this can be one day per line but usually one week per line is enough. What you want to end up with is the amount of their time that is available for the project to use, week by week, for the duration of the project.

1. First talk to each team member and find out when they are on vacation, training courses, or any other activities that will prevent them working on the project

2. Unless they are allocated to the project on a full-time basis, you next need to find out if there are any times that they will not be available because of their day job, for finance people this is often at month end

3. Now fill in the matrix with the number of days they are available for each week

4. Compare this to the amount of their time you have been promised and deal with any shortfalls

Hot tip

Be prepared to escalate any resource shortfalls to your project sponsor.

The Stage Plan

In chapters four and five we looked at developing a project plan, estimate and schedule. Now it's time to take it down one level and produce a Stage Plan which divides a stage into Tasks.

Producing a Stage Plan

It is a good idea to plan each stage, towards the end of the stage before it. That is when we will know the most about it and we need to have the next stage plan, estimate and schedule 'ready to go'.

Back in chapter two we looked at producing an Initiation Stage Plan, so let's move forward and produce a Strategy Stage Plan using the following steps:

1   Start by defining the objectives for the stage, what it has to achieve

2   Next list the deliverables that will need to be produced from the stage

3   Then list the tasks that will have to be carried out to produce the deliverables

4   Now estimate how many days' work effort will be required to complete each task (typically between 3 and 10 days)

If any task is too small (less than one day) see if you can combine it with another task. If any task is too large (over 10 days) then see if you can divide it into two smaller tasks (but remember, they each need to have a deliverable).

Be careful of smaller tasks and don't underestimate them. A one hour meeting is not a one hour task, it is the sum total of the meeting preparation time, the actual time spent at the meeting and any follow-up time (producing notes or minutes).

5   Add a dummy Contingency task to the end of the stage to allow for the things you don't yet know about

Around 10% is usually right for contingency when you are planning the next stage.

Don't forget

Contingency should be profiled with less in the short term and more in the distant future.

Allocating Resources

The next step involves allocating resources to each task. Having identified your resources and established their skills and abilities together with their availability you can now perform the final two steps:

6 Allocate each task to the most appropriate person (or people) to do it

7 Finally plot the tasks onto a Gantt chart, assuming 3½ days work per week per full-time person (this is based on the 180 productive days per year scheduling guideline)

The following example has been produced for the strategy stage of the West Country Tours project:

Don't forget

Allow time to arrange meetings and to get deliverables approved.

Strategy Stage Plan

Objectives
To determine and document the strategic business requirements for the new holiday product.

Key Stage Deliverables
- Approved Strategy Plan
- Next Stage Plan
- End Stage Report

Schedule
The following Gantt Chart illustrates the stage schedule (note the last three tasks have been wrapped around to the left-hand side):

Task Name	Dur	01	02	03	04	05	06	07	08	09	10	11	12	13	14	15	16	17
Schedule interviews	1	▮																
Carry out interviews	3			▮▮▮														
Draft report	2								▮▮									
Present findings	1												▮					
Finalize report	2														▮▮			
Contingency	2																▮▮	
Business sign off	1	▮																
Plan next stage	2		▮▮															
End stage report	2						▮▮											

Hot tip

For legibility, the last three tasks have been wrapped around rather than extended on a further chart to the right.

Organizing Activities

The final step is to divide any large or complex Tasks into detailed Activities (or sub-tasks) and then estimate and schedule them. An activity is the lowest level chunk we want to divide work into and typically it will be between half a day and three days' work effort (although it could be more or less). Ideally it should only be carried out by one person.

Small tasks may not need splitting any further, particularly if they already fit this definition of an activity. In this case just schedule the task.

Working with Activities

Overall there can be a lot of activities in a project (typically around 480 in a small to medium sized project). We have to make sure that each of them happens in the right sequence and that the right person (or other resource) is in the right place, at the right time, to carry it out.

Activities need to be organized at a detailed level, which is normally a time frame of between two and four weeks. At this level we also need to use real days, to take into account holidays and other activities. So rather than scheduling 3.5 days' work effort per week (based on 180 days a year) we use real days but only schedule 4.5 days per full-time equivalent person, per week to allow for some unproductive time.

Creating an Activity List

We create an activity list by carrying out the following steps:

1 Start by identifying the objectives for the task (even tasks can have objectives)

2 Now break the task down into each of the separate activities that will be involved in carrying out the task

3 Estimate the amount of work effort that will be required for each activity (this can be anything from an hour to several days)

4 Finally identify any dependencies between the activities (activities that need another activity to be completed before they can begin)

Remember that one person performs an activity, so if you have two or more people working on a task you will need to identify each of their activities separately so that you can schedule the time for it accurately.

Example Activity List

At the end of the Strategy Stage, it is usual to prepare a report to senior management and present it to them. This is an important task and one for which we can produce a detailed activity list and schedule.

Prepare & Present Report to Management
Objectives

To obtain management approval for the strategic business requirements and proposed method of proceeding.

ID	Activity	Effort	Dependencies
01	Rough out content of report and list of proposed attendees	4 hours	none
02	Discuss with team and agree format of the strategy report	3 hours	01
03	Confirm availability of attendees and book meeting room for presentation and dry run	2 hours	02
04	Review progress of report and update project plan with real times and costs	4 hours	02
05	Produce final strategy report, handouts and slides for presentation	4 hours	04
06	Dry run presentation to team and update material as necessary	4 hours	03 and 05
07	Give presentation to management and ask for approval to proceed	4 hours	03 and 06

As can be seen from the above the task would have been estimated at around 3 to 4 days' work effort. The activities can then be allocated to the appropriate resource and scheduled as we shall see in the next topic.

Activity Schedules

Having produced a list of activities and estimated the work for each (in the previous topic), the next step is to schedule the activities onto a Gantt Chart.

Creating an Activity Schedule

Use a sheet of paper (or project scheduling tool) to create a schedule for your project like this:

Activity	Dur hr	01	02	03	04	05	06	07	08	09	10	11	12	13	14	15	16	17
Rough out content	4	■																
Discuss with team	3		■															
Arrange meeting	2			■														
Review progress	4				■													
Produce report	4					■												
Dry run & changes	4								■									
Presentation	4													■				

1. List the activities down the left-hand side in the sequence in which they need to be carried out

2. Enter the work effort in hours for each task as the duration (which is usually the same at this level)

3. Now plot in the first activity on the appropriate day on the right-hand side of the chart

Each day on the Gantt Chart is an elapsed day, so you need to take into account holidays and any time when people will be away or on other activities. At this level use 4.5 days per week, per person productivity.

4. Now plot in the other activities, making sure that any activities on which they are dependent will have been completed, and allowing sufficient elapsed time for each to be completed

We have now taken the activity list we created in the previous topic and turned it into an activity schedule.

Hot tip

Make sure you allow sufficient elapsed time for each activity to be completed.

Scheduling Activities

When producing an activity list and schedule there are some key questions to ask:

1   Have the objectives of the Task been clearly established and understood?

2   Are any important deadlines known and incorporated into the schedule?

3   Have all the dependencies been identified?

4   Is all the necessary information available?

5   Has the schedule been communicated to and checked with the people who will be carrying out the activities?

Controlled Approach

Organizing the activities in a project can be carried out using the process we have just worked through. Most of the time we should only need to concentrate on one Stage and two or three Tasks at a time. This way we really can stay in control of the project.

Strategic View

As well as operating at this detailed level, the project manager also needs to operate at the strategic level (thinking strategically about the project and its stages). Otherwise you can get lost in the detail. One of the best ways of achieving this is through regular update meetings with your project sponsor.

Hot tip

Concentrate on one stage and two or three tasks at a time to stay organized but don't lose sight of the big picture!

Documentation

Documentation and filing are fairly dry subjects but they are part of the necessary organization of a project. A properly documented project will help the project manager stay in control and manage effectively. It will help to ensure the project deliverables are being produced to the correct level of quality. It will give continuity with people changes on the project. It will help establish the achievement of benefits and provide valuable information for future projects and methods of working.

The Project Manager's Role

The project manager is responsible for setting up and maintaining the project files. They may well delegate the day to day work of keeping files up to date to another team member or a project assistant, but they are still responsible for it. So it is important to set up a proper filing system and document it so that other team members can use it and know where to find things.

Filing Structure

Ideally the project filing structure should be defined, set up and documented during the Initiation Stage. It will need to cover paper filing, electronic filing and filing of any technical or specialist deliverables. One approach is to split project filing into three major types of files. These are the project management files, the specialist or technical files and the quality files. These, together with their suggested content are set out in the following sections.

Beware

Documentation is never a popular topic, but it is a vital one if you are going to stay in control.

118

Hot tip

Document everything in a proper filing system. You'll be glad you did!

Project Management Files

These files should containing all the project documentation. This would include the terms of reference, business case, project initiation document, project plan, project organization chart, job descriptions and the project risk log. There should be a sub-file for each project stage containing the stage plans, work assignments, progress reports, end stage reports and general correspondence.

In addition to the current versions of each of these documents, all previous versions should also be retained. These days most, if not all, of these documents will be electronic, produced using a word processor or spreadsheet program, so care needs to be taken in naming different versions of the same document and potentially retaining signed off paper copies as well.

Specialist Files

Technical deliverables such as requirements documents, computer software and other specialist deliverables need the same level of control and usually some form of configuration management system to track and control changes to them.

Quality File

Finally agreed descriptions for all major deliverables, records of quality checks carried out together with their results and items like the project issue log also need to be filed under quality.

Summary

- Project managers need to be organized if they are going to stay in control of their project

- The best way of organizing a project is by structuring it. This is why we break a project down into stages, then the stages into tasks and so on

- The project team are the key resources on a project and they need to be organized so that they can communicate effectively

- We also need to know what skills and abilities each team member has and when they are available and not available to the project so that we can schedule the work effectively

- The optimum time to develop a project stage plan is just before the stage is due to start. You should have the maximum knowledge of what needs to be done at that time

- We develop a stage plan by defining its objectives, listing the deliverables and then working out the tasks we need to complete to produce them

- It is important to add some contingency into a stage plan as we will not know everything that is going to happen in a stage

- Schedule the tasks onto a Gantt chart and allocate the resources who are going to carry out the work. This is where the skills and availability matrices come in very handy

- The stage plan should document the objectives of the stage, list the deliverables that will be produced, list the tasks that will be carried out and show when they will happen

- Large or critical tasks should be broken down into their constituent activities for greater control and to create an activity list for the task

- Activity schedules are similar to task schedules but take the activity list as their input in place of the task list

- While documentation and filing are fairly dry subjects, they are also essential to the successful organization of a project

8 Leading

This chapter deals with the third key skill, leading. It covers the people involved and the methods of leadership together with the need for effective communication with them.

Stakeholders

Leading is the third of the key project management skills and the project manager certainly needs to lead the project, but who exactly is being led?

In Chapter 2 we looked at project stakeholders and identified three key interest groups: the Business, the Users and the Suppliers. We also looked at some of the things that could go wrong if they are not adequately involved in the project.

The Project Team

Let's assume that we have selected our project team along the suggested lines. We have a team with a vested interest in the success of the project. We also have the backing of top management (through our project sponsor) and are supported by any technical people we may need. Now we can move on to identifying the other stakeholders.

Stakeholder Identification

Take a sheet of paper and draw up a table similar to the one opposite, then carry out the following steps:

1 List all of the stakeholders (or groups of stakeholders) down the left-hand side

2 Think about what each one's expectations might be and enter those in the next column

③ Now consider what the worst possible outcome could be if you don't involve them in the project and enter that in the third column

④ Finally think what the likely implications for the project would be if this were to happen and enter that in the fourth column

The following example shows the results of the exercise for West Country Tours:

Stakeholders	Expectations	Non-involvement	Implications
Business Owners or Directors	Project completed on time, to budget and with all the benefits achieved	Poor understanding of issues and lack of ownership of the business case	Disaster
Staff	Additional business growth and interest but more work	Alienation, lack of support, hostility or even rejection	Disaster
Customers	Holidays work out exactly as they expect with no problems	It might be the wrong product	Disaster
Hotel Owners	Plenty of notice of bookings and a system that is simple to administer	Difficulties with bookings and the booking system	Serious problems
Bike Suppliers	Early notification of exact requirements and good publicity for their bikes	Danger of wrong bikes or lack of availability when required	Serious problem
Printers	Early delivery of text and art work to them, agreement of proofs and no late changes	Missed deadlines or poor quality work	Serious problem

Don't forget

Don't forget your end users and their expectations.

123

From this exercise you should be able to see the likely impact on your project if you don't understand and address all of your stakeholders' expectations. Keep your output from this exercise as we will refer to it again later, when we look at the best way to address these stakeholders' expectations.

The Change Process

They say that change is exciting when you are doing it but threatening when it's being done to you. As project management is the management of change, it is important to understand the impact that change can have on people. The change process can cause uncertainty and anxiety in those affected by it.

There is an adaptation of the bereavement counselling model that can help us to understand the impact of the change process. This identifies four steps to the process: denial, resistance, exploration and acceptance:

1 Denial is the first reaction in some people when they hear about a change. By denying the existence of the change it might just go away, or perhaps the people responsible for the change will begin to think it is a bad idea

2 Resistance is the next step, people will tell you it won't work, or it was tried before and it failed. It can even turn into sabotage as they try to prevent the change from taking place or more subtly try to undermine it

3 Exploration starts once people have got over the resistance phase and have started to accept that the change will happen

4 Acceptance is the final step once the change has actually taken place. People begin to see that the new way actually does work and may even start to prefer it to the old way

By knowing about and understanding these four steps or phases we can deal with them in the appropriate way. The key thing is to get the resistance out into the open so it can be dealt with rather than trying to hush it up.

Commitment

To manage the change process effectively we need commitment from three key groups of people:

- Active and visible top management commitment and support

- The full commitment of the people who will be making the change (the project team)

- Commitment of the people who will be affected by the change (the end users)

The way of obtaining the full commitment from these three key groups is by involving them in the project and communicating:

1 Recognize the emotional response to change in people (as covered on the page opposite)

2 Build commitment to the change by talking to them and, more importantly, by listening to them

3 Support the change process through the provision of training and hands on support at the critical time of change over

Don't forget

Project management is the management of change.

Teamwork

One of the key differences between line management and project management is that project management is all about teamwork. In a normal line management role and environment, the manager tells their people what to do. They hand out the work, they assess the results, they decide how well their people have worked and they approve salary increases and promotion.

Project Management is Different

In projects the project manager is just one member of the team. They don't have direct authority over the other team members but they need them to do the work necessary for the project to succeed.

So the project manager is more like the captain of a sports team, they need to inspire, urge the team on to victory and support them when they get into difficulties. You can go about this by using the following steps:

Beware

If you don't understand the objectives, no one else will!

1. Create a team identity: get the whole team to buy into and agree the common goal (objectives), that you can all agree you are going to achieve

2. Agree how you are going to work together as a team, it won't necessarily be the same way they work in their regular day jobs, so be creative

3. Make sure they each know their role and what they have to do in the project team, which may be totally different from what they do in their normal job

4. Get their commitment; the project is an exciting journey and they can help make it a great project

5. Make it enjoyable; projects are different and more exciting than business as usual, so build on that fact and make sure it's fun as well as a challenge

Do that and you will have a team that works together, wins together and hopefully even plays together when the time is right. You will have a winning team.

Delegation

The other key element in teamwork is delegation. You can't do everything yourself and working in a team you not only have to delegate, you also have to trust the team member you are delegating to. These are the steps to effective delegation:

1 Define what you are delegating: if you can't describe the task then stop, don't delegate it until you can

2 Make sure the person you are delegating to understands exactly what you need them to do

3 Check that the person you are delegating to has the necessary skills and abilities to carry out the task

4 Be there to help them while they are doing it, check from time to time to see if they need any help or guidance

5 Monitor their progress, you are still responsible for the task being completed so don't abandon them

These steps will help you to get the best out of the team. But a team doesn't just happen, it needs to be built and we will look at that in the next topic.

Hot tip

If the person doesn't have all the required skills be prepared to give them a lot of support.

Beware

Try not to micro-manage people as it produces a very negative reaction.

Team Building

Project teams have their own particular dynamics but the theory is that all teams go through four stages of development:

Forming

This is the first stage when you gather the team members together and meet as a team for the first time. They may be excited about the project, they may be worried about it, they may even feel threatened by it. And they may be unsure of you and each other. In short they will be edgy.

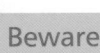
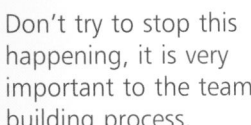

Beware

Don't try to stop this happening, it is very important to the team building process.

Storming

Very soon the team moves into the second stage as they start to examine what the project is trying to achieve and maybe question the objectives. They may have different objectives and this is where the conflicts and arguments will begin as they challenge one another and challenge you.

Norming

Out of the conflicts and arguments, some form of consensus will begin to form as the team starts to make decisions as a team. This is a powerful period and needs careful handling to ensure some members don't feel rejected if their ideas are rejected. But handled carefully it will build the group of people into a real team.

Performing

This is the final stage where the team now functions as a unit and performs well. The team is now working effectively towards achieving its goal.

Support the Team

We have mentioned how important the initial project team "kick off" meeting is several times already. This is where team building starts. If the people are good they will work through the four stages themselves but be aware of where people are in the model and provide support to help them move on to the next stage.

Developing the Team

The initial project team meeting is an excellent opportunity to start the team building process. It should not just be you telling them about the project, it should be about getting them to review and agree your preliminary work. The following steps are a good guide to that process:

1 Review the project objectives with them, get them to talk about what they understand by them and how they map onto their own and their departmental objectives

Beware

Don't just talk at the team, involve them fully in the meeting.

2 Discuss the reasons why the project is happening, this is effectively going through the business case with them, so that they understand why it is important to the business and why the business is prepared to invest their time in it

3 Talk about the results of the project, the benefits it will bring and how it might change the way some people work

4 Discuss other benefits to customers, suppliers and the environment and how it will help the business grow and develop

5 Go through the details of the outline plan and explain why you have planned things the way you have, be prepared to listen and possibly change the plan

Hot tip

Always be prepared to listen to other people's views, they may spot something you missed.

6 Explain their roles and make sure they understand each others' roles

Cover all that and you will have made an excellent "kick off" to the project and a good start to building the team.

129

End Users

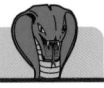

Beware

Forget the end users at your peril.

Someone once referred to the end users as the "forgotten people" as they so often are in projects. So who are the end users and why do they so often get forgotten?

Who Are They?

Put simply, the end users are the people who will use whatever it is that the project will result in. If the project is to implement a new business process it is the staff who will operate that process. If the project is to build a house it is the people who will live in the house.

Identifying the End Users

We need to identify all of the end users impacted by our project so that we can communicate with them. We have to do this because they are going to be affected by the outcome of the project. It is going to change the way they work. Failure to communicate adequately with them will, not unnaturally, cause resistance to change.

Resistance to Change

There are many reasons why people can be resistant to change. Typically, end users could be subject to any one or more of the following:

● Loss of control: change can be very threatening, particularly when you don't know why it is happening and what it will do to the way you currently work

- Surprise: no one likes things being sprung on them with no warning

- Difference: some people are quite happy with the way they currently do things, they may like the old way of working

- Loss of face: they may have helped to create the current processes

- Competence: they may be unsure of their ability to cope with the new way of doing things

- More work: change usually does involve more work, particularly in the short term

- Past resentment: they may have an old, possibly unrelated, grudge that the change gives them a chance to voice

These factors are referred to as 'change inhibitors' and they are all potentially out there among our end users. Therefore, we need to do something to deal with them.

Communication

Once again, it comes back to communication. It really is the only way of dealing with these factors. These are the steps that we need to take:

1. Help them to see the benefits that the new way will bring, either to them or to their customers

2. Provide training so that they feel comfortable and competent with the new way of doing things

3. Talk to all of the people who will be impacted by the change and remember to listen to them too

4. Make them feel involved in the project in some way, by asking their opinion or by getting them to test it

5. Try to identify a 'project champion' in each group, someone who likes the project and who will act as the group focus

Hot tip

It's never too soon to start the communication process.

The Leadership Role

The Project Manager's leadership role is different and requires a slightly different approach at the various stages of the project. This is illustrated, along with some suggestions for the project sponsor, in the following table.

Stage	Project Manager	Project Sponsor
Early	Challenge and verify the objectives	Agree budget and critical success factors
	Team building	Does the project manager need help?
Middle	Identify and resolve any conflicts	Is the project on track?
	Problem fixer	Is the project still on track?
Late	Motivate the team	Motivate the project manager

Objectives

At the start of the project the project manager needs to exercise some leadership in ensuring the objectives are sound. This will mean being prepared to challenge the project sponsor and other senior management if necessary.

Team Building

In the early stages the project manager needs to show leadership in building the new team and getting them working together. To build the team and achieve effectiveness, we need to develop mutual respect and cooperation. Motivating individuals and groups and persuading them to accept responsibility (particularly when not their line manager) requires leadership skills and the ability to:

- Understand people's concerns and fears

- Understand their needs and explain your own

- Get their buy in to the project and to the team

- Thank them for what they do

- Communicate with them

Hot tip

Work on building team spirit by occasionally organizing a fun event. It's a great way to motivate people.

Dealing with Conflict

In the middle stages of a project there will often be tension and differences of opinion about the best way of doing something. This can easily lead to conflicts, which will require leadership from the project manager.

Dealing with Problems

The middle to late stages of a project are usually where the problems come to light. Everything may seem to be going very smoothly and people start to relax and become complacent. No one spots the iceberg on the horizon until there is a sudden impact and the project is in serious danger.

Motivation

The later stages of a project will often involve a lot of hard work for the team. This can easily lead to people getting depressed and demotivated. The project manager therefore needs to use their leadership skills to remotivate them.

There can also be apprehension about what life after the project will be like. People may be worried about going back to their old roles and business as usual after the excitement of the project. Whatever the cause, the project manager will have to use their leadership skills to motivate the team.

All of these skills rely on one underlying principle, the need to communicate with people.

Hot tip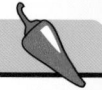

Never stop communicating with your team.

Effective Communications

One of the things we keep coming back to, time after time, is the need for the project manager to communicate. But for that communication to be effective, it must be more than just talking to people. That alone will not achieve effective communication.

It's Not What You Say

When we tell someone something, we don't necessarily communicate what we've intended, but what they have understood us to say. People will put their own interpretation onto things and that is what they will remember, if they remember anything at all!

It is said that people generally only remember:

- 10% of what they read
- 20% of what they hear
- 30% of what they see
- 50% of what they see and hear

So if we have to communicate something that is important, it's not enough just to send a memo or an email.

Get Some Feedback

People will remember things better if they have spoken them as well as having heard them. If we ask them to verify that they have understood something, we also help them to remember it. But, if something is important, it should always be backed up in writing.

Don't forget

It's not what you say when communicating, it's what they hear.

134

Hot tip

When communicating good news, get them to react to it. It's a great way of building team spirit.

Common Understanding

If we have something important to communicate and we want to achieve a common understanding, it makes sense to communicate with people in a group. For the project team this will typically be the team meeting. Then we can make sure there is a common understanding, by getting them to confirm it. If there are differences they can be addressed and, hopefully, everyone will leave the meeting with the same message. All of these aids to effective communication build on each other.

Communication Methods

Oral communication, either one-to-one or in meetings, is only one of the many ways of keeping people in the picture. While it is excellent for important communications, it may not always be practical or we may also want to use other channels to back it up.

Electronic mail is probably the most frequently used (and often abused) communication channel but there are also bulletin boards, blogs, wikis, notice boards and so on. All of these are potentially valid ways of communicating with stakeholders.

Belief

Finally when we communicate, particularly orally, we must believe what we are saying and we must be prepared to show it:

1. Believe in yourself: if you don't you will be unconvincing and no one will believe what you say

2. Believe in the project: if you don't believe in the project you shouldn't be running it

3. Believe in the project team: if you don't they will detect it and you will lose their commitment

4. Believe in success: you must believe the project will succeed, if not it will surely fail

5. Believe what you are saying: if you don't they will know

Do this and you will be communicating effectively, whichever communications channel you use.

Don't forget

Reinforce your oral communication: tell them what you are going to say, say it and then tell them what you told them.

Communications Plan

Having produced a list of project stakeholders and identified their expectations earlier in this chapter, we should now be in a position to put together a communication plan for the project.

Producing the Plan
Using a sheet of paper divided into three columns, similar to the example on the right, carry out the following steps:

1 List all the people and groups of people that you need to communicate with down the left-hand column (this should be similar to your list of stakeholders but you may wish to combine or split some groups)

2 In the middle column list the things that you will need to communicate to each person or group to satisfy their interests in the project and keep them informed

3 In the right-hand column identify how you are going to communicate (email, one-to-one, team meeting, presentation, etc.) bearing in mind that it may require more than one channel of communication to be effective

That gives you a communication plan to start with. But it will not be static and you should expect it to change during the course of the project, as stakeholders' expectations change and you identify new stakeholders.

Keep It Up To Date
Communication plans need to be reviewed and updated on a fairly regular basis. Keep asking what needs to be communicated and to whom. Or better still, have a standard item on the project meeting agenda to cover communication, that way you can involve the rest of the team in the exercise as well.

Don't Stop
Don't ever stop communicating. We need to keep on reminding people about the project, why we are doing it, what it is going to achieve, what's currently happening and why.

Remember to follow up your oral communications in writing, particularly if they are important or if you want people to remember things or take actions based on them.

Hot tip

Review your communications plan on a regular basis.

Example Communication Plan

The following example is the communication plan for our South West Tours project:

Who	What	How
(the people you will communicate with)	(the sort of information that you will need to communicate to them)	(the method and frequency of these communications)
Business Owners and Directors	Progress against time and budget and any issues or problems	Regular briefings and agreed issue escalation process
Staff	What we are doing on the project, why and regular progress updates	Briefings and meetings initially, then monthly updates
Customers	What we are planning to provide them and when	Mail shots and possibly surveys
Hotel Owners	Details of how the booking process will work and when	Meetings to start, then regular updates plus involve them in the project
Bike Suppliers	Expected routes (type of terrain), numbers, type of holiday maker and timings	Initial meetings then regular updates plus involve them in the project
Printers	What we will need, when and the quality we are expecting	Initial meetings, regular updates and involve in the project

Don't forget

Don't forget the end users.

The above plan is based on the stakeholders identified in the example at the start of the chapter. It attempts to address their expectations and involve them in the project. Hopefully this will then prevent the risk of the identified cost of non-involvement and consequent implications for the project.

Difficult People

If we involve our team, communicate with them and do all the other team building things, we should have established good morale and got the team functioning effectively. But there will almost certainly be conflicts from time to time and we must not let them divide the team.

Differences of Opinion

Firstly, there is nothing wrong with people in the project team having different views or opinions. In fact, it can be quite beneficial and help the team dynamics. If everyone is in total agreement about everything, it would be a pretty static team and lack any creative spark. But the project manager has to control and channel it, and that can mean having to deal with difficult situations and difficult people.

Dealing with Difficult People

Dealing with difficult people could be the subject of a book in its own right. We have already covered some of the key issues involved such as:

- the need to negotiate with people rather than just telling them what to do

- being open and honest in your dealings with them

- expecting them to be open and honest with you in return

Guidelines

As a project manager we must be prepared to deal with difficult people, or we will lose our credibility. The following steps represent a proven technique to follow:

1 Try to identify what is actually causing the difficulty, it may not be obvious to start with

2 Make sure it is not something that you have or haven't done

3 Try to be quietly assertive and make sure you don't over react

4 Decide where you want to get to, whether you want to turn their behavior round or just get rid of them

5 If you do want to try and keep them on the project, tell them how important it is to you and explain what you need them to do to rectify the situation

6 If that doesn't work, make sure you don't give them anything critical to the project, you need to get them off the critical path

7 Finally, if all else fails, get them off the project before they can damage it

This sounds tough and it is, but in the end, it is the only way of stopping them damaging your project.

Beware

Never get aggressive with difficult people, that's what they want!

Hot tip

If they are not prepared to help, get rid of them.

Senior People

Just to make matters worse, what happens if the person causing the difficulty in the project is senior to you in the organization?

This shouldn't make any difference. A senior person can probably cause even more damage to the project than a more junior person, so the same steps apply. But a word of caution, before embarking on them you would be advised to have a word with your project sponsor, they may well be able to assist.

Summary

- Stakeholders are all those people with a vested interest in the outcome of a project and they need to be identified, their expectations need to be understood along with the likely implications of not involving them in the project

- Projects involve change and the change process can be very threatening to people if they are not fully involved. We need to recognize this emotional response, build commitment to the change and support them through the change

- Teamwork is the key to an effective project team and the project manager, as captain of the team, needs to build commitment and trust through the process of delegation

- Teams go through four phases of development: Forming, Storming, Norming and Performing and the project manager can ease this process by supporting the team through it

- The initial project team kick off meeting is an excellent place to start the team development by involving the team members in it fully

- End users are the people who will be most affected by the project and they may well be very resistant to it. The way to deal with this is through a process of communication

- The leadership role requires different things at different times in a project: early on you will need to challenge the objectives and build the team, in the middle stages you will need to deal with conflicts and fix problems, in the later stages you will need to keep the team motivated

- Make sure your communication is effective by using the most appropriate method and believe in yourself, the project, the project team, success and what you are saying

- Develop a communication plan to address the expectations of the project stakeholders, listing who you will communicate with, what you will communicate and how

- Difficult people have to be dealt with or they will harm the project. Try to find out the cause of the difficulty, make sure it's not something you've done, be assertive, try to get them to change their behavior but if all else fails get rid of them

9 Controlling

Controlling is the fourth key skill area for project managers. In this chapter we look at the various techniques for staying in control of the project.

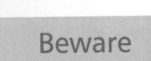
Keeping Control

Clearly we need to make sure we stay in control of our projects and keep them on course. But exactly how do we do that?

Project Control Loop

The following diagram illustrates the key elements involved in the project control loop:

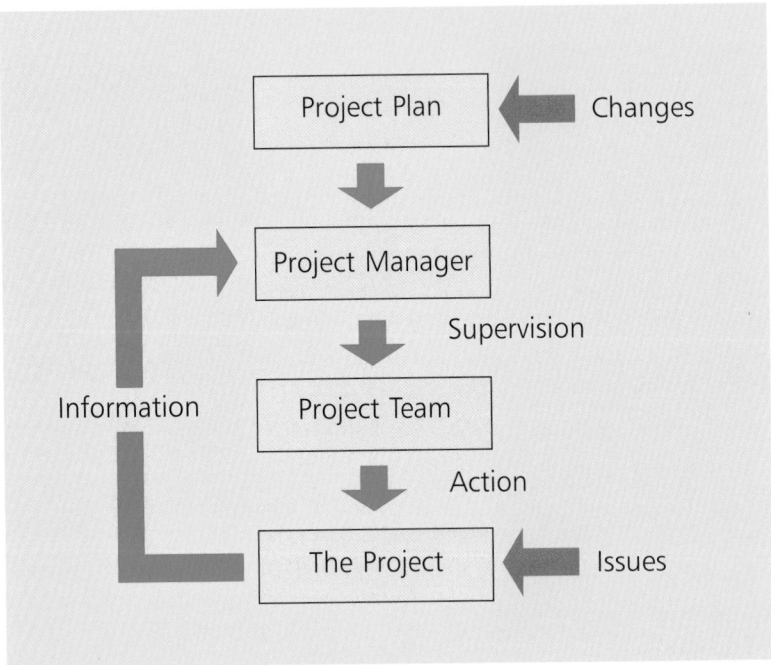

Project Plan

Everything starts out from the project plan, as illustrated above. The plan documents what is supposed to happen on the project and is the benchmark against which things are measured.

Project Manager

The project manager takes the plan as input and then allocates the work out to the project team. The project manager then supervises the team to ensure that they carry it out.

Project Team

The individual team members accept these assignments of work and carry them out. This will include the project manager, as they will usually be doing some of the work on the project in addition to project managing it.

The Project

In order to complete these work assignments the team members will take the necessary action to get the project done. So that is the first part of the model working down from the plan to completing the project.

But to keep in control of the project, the project manager needs to know what is actually happening and for that they need information.

Information

The project manager needs a continual flow of information back about the project in order to track that it is on schedule and to budget. If it is, then the project is in control but if it is not then the project is getting out of control and the project manager will need to initiate some actions. But there are other things that can cause problems and these are referred to generically as issues.

Issues

Project issues are the things that happen on the project that are not part of the plan. Perhaps something will not be ready by the time it is needed. Maybe something doesn't work the way it was supposed to. Perhaps a key member of the team has got a serious illness and can't work. These are all project issues and the project manager needs to know about them.

Changes

The final piece of the model are the changes that can impact on the project plan. For example someone senior may decide that the business requirements have changed or perhaps due to adverse trading conditions the budget must be reduced. These are the types of thing that can impact on the plan and therefore the project.

Keeping in Touch

The project manager needs to have a way of keeping track of all these things to stay in control of the project. You could chase around having one to one meetings with everyone on the project team, getting continual updates on where they are with their work, but it would not be a very good use of your time. We need to keep in touch with everyone, on an informal basis, but we also need something a bit more formal. And the best way of doing that is through regular team meetings.

Hot tip

Make sure you get back a continual flow of information on how the project is going.

143

Don't forget

As well as informal contact with the team, we need regular team meetings.

Project Meetings

We saw earlier in the book that project meetings are important for team building and communicating. We also saw in the previous topic that they are important for helping the project manager stay in control of the project.

Project Team Meetings

The team meetings are a chance to get everyone involved in the project together. Naturally you want to review progress, but they are also an opportunity to recognize achievements, discuss problems and areas of mutual concern and get the whole team working together.

Effective Meetings

To be effective, project team meetings need to be relatively formal, with agenda and minutes:

- They should start on time, get on with the business and make decisions

- They need to be controlled, so as not to waste people's time

- They need to be regular, ideally weekly or every two weeks at least

It is a good idea to schedule them for the same time and day of the week, every week. Then everyone can book the time in their diary and it saves having to arrange each one individually.

Hot tip

If you schedule a meeting every week, you can always cancel one if it's not needed.

Agenda

Meetings should focus on reviewing progress. Activities, tasks or stages that have been completed, since the last meeting, should be recognized. Problems or issues that have occurred, can be addressed. Information that team members need to pass on can be communicated. And the plan for the period ahead can be formulated and agreed. The following is a typical project team meeting agenda.

South West Tours Project Team Meeting

Date: Every Wednesday
Time: 2 PM to 3 PM
Location: Project Meeting Room

Agenda

1. Introduction

2. Tasks & Deliverables Completed

3. Tasks & Deliverables Not Completed

4. Issues

5. Actions

6. Plan for the Next Week

7. Any Other Business

Beware

Make sure every team member has a chance to speak or they will feel left out of the meeting and lose interest.

145

Minutes

Minutes don't have to be formal and they should be structured the same as the above agenda. Any introductory remarks followed by a list of the things completed. Then a list of things that should have been completed but weren't, with a brief reason why. Then a list of any issues that have been identified. The action section is a key section as it should list what is going to be done about the issues and late deliverables. The plan for next week reminds everyone what new tasks and deliverables are about to become due, a timely reminder.

Hot tip

Get your minutes out by email the same day if possible, then no one has an excuse for forgetting anything.

Measuring Progress

In order to keep control and measure progress, we need some form of checkpoints or milestones in the project. These can be major or minor events.

From the project sponsor's perspective, the project stages and, in particular, the end stage reviews represent the major milestones in the project. They should be less concerned with the tasks and deliverables, which to them are minor activities. However, from the project manager's perspective every deliverable should be a milestone while the detailed tasks and sub-tasks are the minor activities.

Percent Completion

One of the most frequently used measures of progress is the percentage completed or how much of the work has been done. The following example is from a real, four-month duration, project that was measured by how much work had been done.

Project Progress	
January	25% complete
February	50% complete
March	75% complete
April	90% complete
May	95% complete
June	98% complete

What the example shows is how the percentage complete measure breaks down in real life. Say the project had been estimated at 60 days' work effort and scheduled to take four months.

- at the end of January 15 days' work had been done

- at the end of February 30 days' work had been done

- at the end of March 45 days' work had been done

- at the end of April 60 days' work had been done but the project was not completed and so on...

Optimism
One major indication of project failure has been identified as inaccurate reporting. This can manifest itself as the '80% complete' syndrome (when asked about the progress of a task an optimist will frequently say "80% complete").

The way to prevent this happening is to base progress recording on full completion of a task and that means the relevant deliverable has been produced (and approved or accepted). Until then the full estimate for the task should remain outstanding.

Given that the average size of a Task is around 5 days, this is not carrying too heavy a burden of 'unrecognized' work and, if work needs to be redone (which is not unknown), the time required is still in the schedule.

Verifiable Measurement
Using this approach, progress is measured by the completion of deliverables. When all the deliverables in a stage have been completed the stage is completed. When all the stages have been completed the project is completed. There is no measurement of partial completion, so we are avoiding the problem of optimism. Many projects could have been saved from disaster, if they had implemented this simple rule.

Reviewing Progress
When reviewing progress the project manager should consider a task to be in one of three states: not started, started or completed. This should then be documented, with the person who it is allocated to, any problems or issues they are having and the actions to be taken to deal with them.

 Beware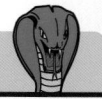

If you measure progress by the amount of work done, you could be in for a nasty surprise.

147

Project Reports

Project reports form a key control mechanism and provide a vital record of what happened during a project. The main reports to be produced are progress reports, time sheets, end stage reports, exception reports and the end project report.

Time Sheets

Never popular but every person working on a project should complete a weekly time sheet recording the amount of time they spent on each of the tasks they have been allocated. They should also estimate the amount of work remaining to complete the task.

Progress Reports

A weekly project progress report, circulated to the project team, records progress at the detailed level. If you are holding weekly project team meetings and producing minutes or some other record of the meetings, that will be your weekly progress report. It should contain the same sections as the agenda. At the end of a stage and at the end of a project you will be able to go back and review exactly what happened on a week by week basis.

Project Status Reports

A monthly project status report should be produced for the project sponsor. This should be in a similar format to the weekly progress reports but slightly more strategic and not containing as much detail. The project sponsor should be interested in the 'big picture' not the detail. An example report is shown opposite.

End Stage Reports

As the name suggests these reports are produced at the end of each stage to summarize how the stage worked out in practice as compared to the stage plan. This is covered in Stage Boundaries later in this chapter.

Exception Reports

These are used to document any events that will take a project outside of its time or budget constraints. It should describe the problem, what caused it to happen and the impact it has had or will have on the project. It should then set out the alternatives for dealing with the problem, the costs, risks and any other impact they might have together with the project manager's recommendation for which option to take. This report should then be submitted to the project sponsor or steering committee for a final decision.

Beware

If you don't record the actual time spent on tasks, you'll never know whether your estimates are accurate or not.

Hot tip

A golden rule for status reports is no surprises. If there is bad news tell your project sponsor in person.

Project Status Report

Introduction

This report covers progress on the project for the month of February.

Budget Status

Expenditure on the project as at the end of February was $1,220 against a planned expenditure of $1,500. The forecast final expenditure is $15,000 in line with the budget.

Human resource usage to date is 40 days against the budget of 45 days and this reflects the non-availability of one member of the project team due to illness.

Schedule Status

The project is currently around three days behind schedule, due to the absence of one member of the team. This is well within the agreed tolerance and the time should be caught up by the end of the current stage.

Deliverables Completed

- stage plan issued
- interviews completed
- draft strategy report issued

Issues and Risks

Currently there are no project issues. There are 22 risks open in the risk log, but none of these are significant nor do they require any action from the project sponsor.

Deliverables Planned

- presentation of findings
- strategy report finalized & signed off by the business
- end stage report

Change Impact

No project changes were requested or approved.

End Project Report

Finally at the end of the project the project manager should produce the end project report. This will set out what happened on the project, compared to the original project plan. It will also identify the lessons learned during the project and any recommendations for future actions.

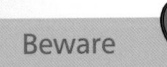

Change Control

Project management is the management of change but it is essential that changes to the project happen in a controlled way. If not, they can be one of the major causes of project failure.

The Impact of Change

The first thing to recognize about change is that it will always have an impact on the project. That impact may be good if the change results in a simplification or reduction of requirements. But it is more likely to be adverse and it is worth considering the following model:

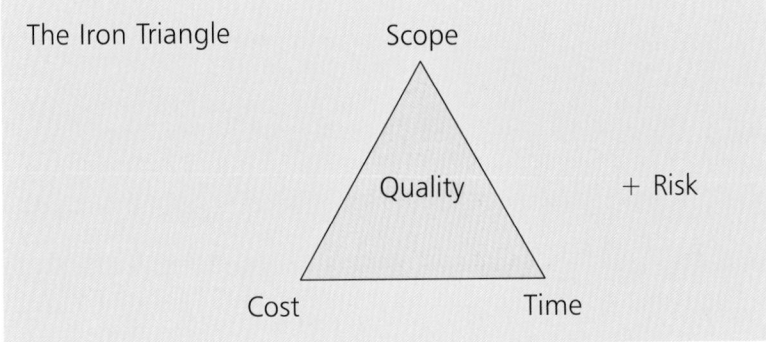

The Iron Triangle was originally defined to show the links between project scope, cost and time. Put simply, any change to the scope of the project must have an impact on the time it takes to complete it or the cost of doing so (possibly both). Similarly any change to the time (say bringing forward the completion date) must have an impact on the cost (increasing it) or the scope (reducing what can be done). Finally any reduction in budget will reduce the scope or increase the time it takes.

Quality and Risk

More recently Quality was added to the model as any change to the scope, cost or time that does not have counterbalancing adjustments made to the other two will have an impact on the quality of the results of the project. The final factor to recognize is that change will always increase risk.

Business Requirements

When considering change, the prime project deliverable is the Business Requirements document. It should be the source of everything that is subsequently done in the project.

The business requirements are first identified and documented during the Strategy Stage. They are then expanded in the Analysis Stage. After that the project will be looking for the best way of meeting those requirements and then implementing the solution to the requirements.

Traditionally the requirements would be 'frozen' at the end of the Analysis Stage and ideally no changes would be made until the project was completed. Unfortunately in the real world that approach has proved to be unworkable.

Reasons for Change

There can be many reasons for a change:

- Someone changed their mind

- There is a new business or legal requirement

- New technology has emerged that should be used

- Someone just thought of a better way of doing something

- Or something we never thought of has just happened

During the Design and Build Stage, while the project team are identifying potential solutions, it is not uncommon to realize that a requirement was misstated or missed altogether. Even when we are building the solution, it is not unusual for some technical or implementation consideration to force us to go 'back to the drawing board'.

Controlling Changes

Every new (or changed) requirement that is identified, needs to be documented and controlled. The inclusion of contingency (sometimes actually referred to as a change budget) in the estimate for each stage is intended to allow for additional or changed requirements that are later identified.

The key decision is, which of these new or changed requirements should be included in the project and which requirements may have to be dropped or demoted to allow their inclusion. Any changes that would take the project outside its time frame, reduce the business functionality being delivered (scope or quality) or increase the costs, will need to get the formal approval of the project sponsor.

Hot tip

Details of what should be produced from each stage of the project are given in the next chapter.

151

Don't forget

Expect changes and plan for them.

Dealing with Change

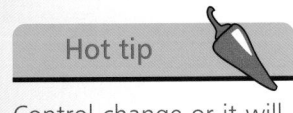

As we saw in the previous topic, any change will have an effect on scope, time or cost (if not all three). At the very least, it will mean some work having to be redone, at worst it could mean a lot of additional work. This topic sets out a formal method for dealing with change.

Project Issues

Any change should start life as a Project Issue. These can be raised by anyone connected with the project. The issue may be a question, a concern, a request for a change or a report of something being wrong. Whichever it is, it should be treated in the same way and recorded in the Issue Log.

Issue Log

The project Issue Log is similar to the project Risk Log and it is not unknown for risks to turn into issues (and vice-versa). It forms a record of every issue raised and what has been done about it. Initially it should record a reference number for the issue, the name of the person raising it and a brief description of the issue.

Priority & Allocation

Each issue needs to have a priority allocated, a decision made about any action that needs to be taken and who is responsible for it. A straightforward question or concern can be dealt with, the answer communicated back to the originator, the details updated in the Issue Log and the issue closed. If an issue is not a straightforward one, it is quite likely to become a request for change.

Change Requests

There are two types of change request, a straightforward request for something to be changed or an off-specification:

- A request for change is anything that will require a change to a previously agreed deliverable such as the Business Requirements

- An off-specification is where a fault has been found in a completed deliverable such as a specification

Traditionally the approach was: if it's off-specification then it has to be fixed, but if it's a request for a change then the answer is no. However, this is not a sensible business approach.

A request for change may have a significant benefit, while a mistake in a document, or a missing bit of function, may have no impact at all. Therefore, it makes sense for all change requests to be subject to the same decision making process:

1 Carry out an impact analysis to identify exactly what would have to be changed

2 Estimate the work effort required to make the change, the cost of making the change and the potential impact on the schedule

3 Check if there will be any impact on the business case and identify any risks associated with making the change

4 Then in the light of all that information, make the business decision as to whether or not the change should be made

Business Decision

As the decision is a business decision, it should be made by the project sponsor (representing the business). They may have delegated responsibility for some level of change to the project manager and if so, the project manager can make the decision, if the change is within their agreed level of authority and they are happy to make it. Otherwise the decision should rest with the project sponsor. In this case the project manager should still make their recommendations to the project sponsor, but it is the sponsor who has the ultimate business responsibility.

Hot tip

Even if you can make the decision, it's wise to discuss it with your project sponsor as well.

Stage Boundaries

The project stages represent the strategic (top-level) view of the project. While the project manager needs to get down into the detail during the stage, dealing with the tasks and deliverables, he or she also needs to operate at the strategic level. This is the level that the project sponsor operates on, so the stage boundaries are the natural point where they can share this strategic focus.

The stage boundaries are the major milestones in a project and should be treated as firebreaks. They provide formal checkpoints, which will allow a project in danger of turning into a runaway train to be stopped in time.

Hot tip

The stage boundaries give you the chance to reappraise your project, use them.

1. The first thing to do is review progress and see how the project has worked out so far. What has worked well and where have there been problems

2. Then compare the actual results to the plan: what should have been completed by now and what have we actually achieved; how much work effort has actually been used compared to the estimate; and what has the project actually cost compared to budget

3. Once the actual cost of the project so far is known, the business case can be updated with it, any variances examined and the reasons identified

Finally we should review the number of change requests, the number accepted and the impact they have had

Once we have reviewed and understood how the project has gone so far, we can look forward with more certainty.

Forward Plan

We can now start planning the next stage. Does anything need to be added as a result of what we now know? Is there anything that will need to be done differently from the way we first planned it? These are the types of questions that need to be asked as the plan for the next stage is developed.

Once we've produced the next Stage Plan, it needs to be reflected up to the project level and the whole Project Plan reviewed. And finally the business case and risks should be reviewed.

End Stage Report

The results of the review and the forward plan are then used to put together the End Stage Report containing:

- The current stage plan with actual and variances

- The project plan for the remainder of the project

- A review of the business case and risks

- A review of any issues and change requests

- The project manager's comments

This report, in draft form, then goes to the project sponsor and forms the basis for the end stage review.

End Stage Reviews

The purpose of the review (either formal or informal) with the project sponsor is to confirm that everything has been completed, as planned, on the project. The discussions and any decisions taken should be noted, along with the formal decision to continue with the project as planned, or to revise the project scope, or even to stop the project. This can then be added to the end stage report, which can then be finalized and issued. The stage is then closed and the next stage of the project starts.

Summary

- In order to keep in control of a project you need a flow of information back from the project team on what is actually happening and any issues that they encounter

- The best way of keeping in touch and getting the information you need is through project team meetings

- Team meetings should be regular, controlled so as not to waste people's time and with a formal or informal agenda and minutes

- The best way of measuring progress is through the completion of deliverables

- Percentage completed is an inaccurate way of measuring progress and subject to the 80% complete syndrome

- All members of the team should complete time sheets with the time spent by task and estimate of work remaining

- Weekly progress reports should document the detailed work of the project for the project team

- Monthly project status reports summarize progress for the project sponsor

- End stage reports document the results of each stage of the project

- Exception reports document any events which will cause a project to exceed its budget or overrun on time, with the options available and the project manager's recommendations

- The end project report documents the final results of the project with any recommendations for future action

- Change will happen so it is best to expect it to happen and have a controlled process in place for dealing with it

- Before making a change carry out an impact assessment estimating the work, cost and impact on schedule of the change

- At the end of each stage produce your end stage report and hold an end stage review with the project sponsor

10 Project Stages

This chapter deals with the project stages, the high-level building blocks that make up the project. It begins with the project life cycle and number of stages. It then provides a list of typical tasks and deliverables for each project stage.

Project Life Cycle

Throughout this book we have referred to and used five project stages for consistency. The full project life cycle consists of these five stages together with project start up and project closure. These are illustrated on the project road map opposite.

Project Start Up
The project start up procedure was covered in chapter two: Getting Started. In summary it is about getting everything prepared for the project to start.

Initiation Stage
The initiation stage was covered and referred to in a number of chapters. The two main reasons for the initiation stage are to get the project team working and to plan the project.

Strategy Stage
The strategy stage is where we define the strategic business requirements. What the business really wants the project to deliver.

Analysis Stage
In the analysis stage we start to identify what will have to be done in order to meet the business requirements. We also start to think about how we will implement what the project will deliver.

Design & Build Stage
This is where the detailed work of the project is carried out. First we design how we will meet the business requirements and then we proceed to build the necessary products and systems to do it. At the end of the design and build stage everything should be ready to go.

Implementation Stage
During implementation we bring the new processes or procedures we have designed and built into use. We train the staff who will be using them and we provide them with support while we cut over to the new way of doing things.

Project Closure
Once we have completed all the deliverables in the implementation stage, including any initial support to the end users, we move into project closure. This is where we gather the lessons learned and pass them over to the organization.

Beware

Once the project is completed, close it down. Don't be tempted to keep trying to improve on things.

Project Road Map

Project Start Up	To start the project in a controlled way: select the team, produce the terms of reference and plan the initiation stage.
Initiation Stage	To plan the project: confirm the business case, develop the plan, document the risks and issues and produce the project initiation document.
Strategy Stage	To determine the strategic business requirements: gather the information, document the strategy and agree it with management.
Analysis Stage	To define what needs to be done: review options and existing systems, develop detailed requirements and implementation strategy.
Design & Build Stage	To design how it will be done and carry it out: create design documents, agree with management and put it into place.
Implementation Stage	To implement and hand over the finished product: train the users, test new systems, bring into production use and hand them over.
Project Closure	To close the project down in a controlled way: complete and hand over the documentation.

Hot tip

At the end of each stage review how the stage went and plan the next one.

Why Five Stages?

Some small or very straightforward projects may not require all five stages. In fact, short projects may only require three stages: Initiation, Design & Build and Implementation. In practice, however, it is often the wrong stages that get dropped. Let's work backwards through the stages, to see if we can knock any out.

Implementation Stage
Most people would agree that a project has to be completed and handed over to the business. The business is responsible for running the new product or process and the Implementation Stage is a convenient way of grouping together all the things involved in the hand over. It is essential, in one form or another.

Design & Build Stage
The Design part involves working out how the new product, system or process is going to be brought into use. The Build part consists of carrying out the work defined by the design. The new product, system or process will be produced or purchased. Quite often this part of the project will be contracted out but it will be required in some form or another. It is where the project work gets done.

Analysis Stage
The purpose of the Analysis Stage is to define what will need to be done in order to meet the business needs (as defined and documented during the strategy stage).

For a larger project this could involve a substantial amount of work and should be retained as a separate stage. For smaller projects, it is possible to combine the analysis stage with either the strategy stage or the design and build stage.

If it is combined with the strategy stage, it involves determining the needs of the business and what will need to be done to satisfy them. If combined with the design and build stage it would involve defining what needs to be done, how it is going to be done and then doing it.

Strategy Stage

The real purpose of the Strategy Stage is to make sure the project team has a full and complete understanding of the business requirements, and that the business has a full and complete understanding of what the project team is going to do. The reason for keeping this relatively short stage is to make sure that understanding exists and is documented.

Initiation Stage

We have already set out the reasons for the Initiation Stage (in Chapter 2) but, to reiterate, it is the first formal stage of the project. We use it to confirm the business case and plan the rest of the project. It also serves to get the project team up and running.

So, while all five of the Project Stages may not always be necessary, the stages that should not be dropped are the Initiation and Strategy Stages. A major cause of failure in projects has been traced back to the decision not to bother with Initiation and Strategy stages. Most of these started straight into the Analysis Stage. But some even skipped the Analysis Stage as well, and started with Design & Build (the "Just Do It" school of thought). It is highly likely that they didn't even recognize the need for these early stages, and weren't aware of the reasons for them.

Typically, what happened was the business requirements got completely missed or misunderstood. This resulted in the need for substantial reworking in the later stages of the project (at the end of Build Stage, if they were lucky, or during the Implementation Stage if that was when the end users got first sight of it). In the worst cases it resulted in the whole project having to be abandoned.

What's in a Name?

Finally however many stages you decide to have, you will need to call them something. If these stage names seem appropriate then use them, if not change them to something more meaningful to you and your organization.

Beware

Make sure you understand the real purpose of each stage before you consider dropping any of them.

Hot tip

Pick stage names that are meaningful to you and your organization.

The Early Stages

Beware

Don't cut corners early in the project, you will pay for it later.

In the past, a large number of projects were carried out that did not include one or more of these early stages. Most of the time, these projects ran into difficulties, often serious difficulties, and usually late in the project. The reasons were fairly obvious. They didn't have clear enough project objectives, they didn't have a clear enough statement of the business requirements, or they hadn't agreed them with the business.

These are all things that the early stages are designed to deal with and ensure there is full agreement between the project team and the business. There is an even more compelling reason for addressing these issues early in the project, it's called Fagan's Law (after M E Fagan of IBM).

Fagan's Law

This states that the effort expended in resolving an issue, varies exponentially, according to the period of time that elapses, before the issue is addressed.

Hot tip

If your business needs convincing about this approach, this diagram may do the trick.

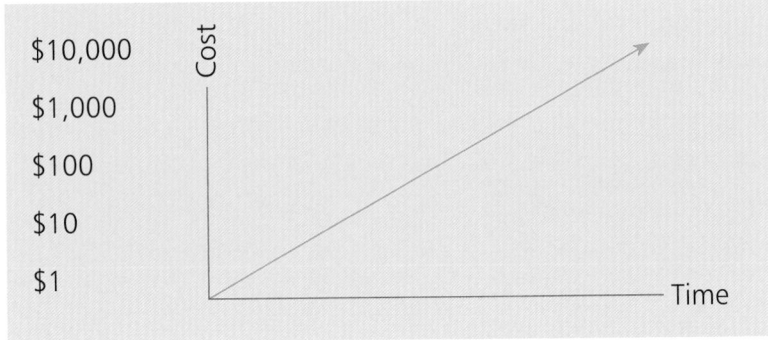

Put another way, to resolve an issue during the Initiation Stage might only take a minute, to resolve it during the Strategy Stage might take 10 minutes, during the Analysis Stage a couple of hours, during the Design & Build Stage it could be anything from a couple of weeks to a couple of months. If it only comes to light during Implementation, you could, potentially, be talking about re-working large amounts of work with consequent delays or even scrapping the project.

So there really is no excuse for not carrying out an Initiation Stage and Strategy Stage. They are both relatively short, compared to the remainder of the project. Not only that, but statistically, projects that include them are more successful than those that don't. Let's look at what they achieve.

Initiation Stage

In small to medium sized projects (the main target of this book) the Initiation Stage, typically, takes around five to ten days' work effort. At the end of it there is a clear 'Go/No Go' business decision. If the decision is 'No Go', then the business has saved itself a significant amount of effort and cost in reaching the correct business decision.

Strategy Stage

The Initiation and Strategy Stages together still represent 10% or less of the total work effort of the project. The Strategy Stage results in a key deliverable: a clear statement of business requirements. This has to be accepted by the business and is again a 'Go/No Go' business decision.

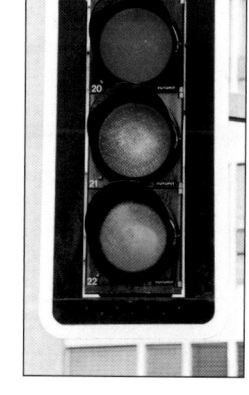

So even if the Initiation and Strategy Stages are completed and a 'No Go' decision is made, the business has not invested heavily, in cost or people's time, to reach that decision. If the decision is 'Go', then the business can move ahead with the project, confident in the knowledge that the project team has a good understanding of the business requirements.

Analysis Stage

The Analysis Stage is often the largest single stage in a project, in terms of work effort. It is where the hard, decision-making work of the project gets done, but still without a really heavy cost to the business. At the end of it the business can see, through detailed proposals, what will have to be done to achieve its requirements. But the business has not yet been disrupted and again, if things have now changed, the business can decide to stop the project, without any real impact on the business.

Once past the Analysis Stage, we are into the detailed work of carrying out the project, through to implementation and beyond. If the early stages have been carried out properly, the project will have a significantly higher chance of success.

Hot tip

Don't be tempted to skip these early stages, they are where the success of the project is built.

Initiation Stage

The primary purpose of the Initiation Stage is to plan the project and confirm the business case. It should be a short stage and will not normally exceed two to three weeks duration.

Stage Deliverables

The deliverables produced will usually include:

- Project Plan: defines how (and when) the project's objectives are to be achieved, showing the major deliverables, tasks and resources required to achieve them

- Business Case: documents the justification for the project, based on the estimated cost and expected business benefits

- Risk Log: a summary record of all identified project and business risks, with their current status

- Communication Plan: defines the parties with an interest in the project and the means of communicating with them

- Project Initiation Document: defines the project and how it will be carried out

- End Stage Report: a summary of progress to date and recommendations on what should happen next

- Next Stage Plan: defines how and when the next stage's objectives are to be achieved, by showing the major deliverables, tasks and resources required to achieve them

Beware

Starting a project without adequate preparation has been likened to building a bridge from A to B; with no agreement on where A is and the sure certainty that B will have moved by the time you get there.

Stage Tasks

Tasks in the Initiation Stage tend to be fairly small. In fact, they can often be treated as Activities (with the Initiation Stage treated almost as a single Task). The following are the typical Tasks

1 Produce the initial project plan (this was covered in some detail in chapter four: Planning and chapter five: Scheduling)

2 Update the Business Case (as covered in chapter three) to reflect the project plan and update the Risks (as covered in chapter six) with any that have been introduced

3 Produce the Communications Plan (as covered in chapter eight: Leading)

4 Set up the Project Controls (as covered in chapter nine), defining how you will control the project and report on progress

5 Set up Project Files (as covered in chapter seven: Organizing) including electronic and paper files

6 Based on all of the above, the Project Initiation Document (PID) can now be assembled (the PID is covered in the next topic)

7 Produce the Stage Plan for the next stage (this was dealt with in chapter seven: Organizing)

8 Present the Findings to Management and obtain approval and funding for the project to continue

In addition to the above it is worth including a dummy task (Project Administration) to cover the general work of managing and administering a project. Although it does not have a formal deliverable it should include time for project meetings and reviews, the production of project reports and all the day to day overheads of managing a project.

Hot tip

If you need to account for your time as project manager, you should include administration in every stage.

Project Initiation Document

The Project Initiation Document (PID) is developed from the terms of reference and documents how the project will be run. It is used as the basis for the decision to authorize the project and should contain the following sections:

Background
To put the project in context, explain how the current position was arrived at and why the project is required.

Project Definition
What the project needs to achieve. This should include the project objectives, scope, method of approach (how you are going to go about the project), main project deliverables, exclusions, constraints and any interfaces.

Assumptions
Any assumptions (particularly planning assumptions) that have been made need to be stated. This will often be around the availability of certain key resources at set times in the project.

Business Case
The outline Business Case should have been refined during the Initiation Stage to reflect the project plan and revised cost estimates.

Project Organization Structure
The structure of the project team, as appropriate to the size of the project and any organizational standards. It should of course also be agreed with the project sponsor.

Communications Plan
Who needs to be communicated with, what their needs are, how they will be communicated with and how frequently.

Quality Plan
Explaining how quality will be managed in the project and any tools to be used for quality assurance. It should cover responsibilities, standards, quality criteria to be applied to key deliverables and quality control. It should also define any audit procedures that will apply to project management and any specialist work. Finally it should deal with any change management and configuration management procedures that will be used.

Beware

Make sure you have documented all your assumptions. If not they may come back to haunt you.

Initial Project Plan
Showing how and when the project activities will occur.

Project Controls
How control is going to be exercised within the project, together with the reporting and monitoring mechanisms to be used.

Exception Process
To explain the process that will be followed if and when an exception (something outside the plan) occurs.

Initial Risk Log
This should document the results of the risk analyses and risk management activities that have taken place so far in the project.

Contingency Plans
Explaining how the consequence of any identified risks that do materialize will be dealt with.

Project Filing Structure
To define how, and where, the information and deliverables produced by the project, are to be filed and retrieved.

As noted above, much of the information will come from the Terms of Reference, with the remainder created during the Initiation Stage. The better the Terms of Reference are, the less the work that will need to be done during the Initiation Stage.

In addition to being the source for obtaining approval for the remainder of the project, the PID should also be a point of reference during future decision making. It is a useful document for anyone joining the project in future.

Hot tip

The PID is probably the single most important document produced in the early stages of a project.

Strategy Stage

The prime purpose of the Strategy Stage is to carry out a more detailed study of the business requirements and why they matter to the business. These are then communicated back to the business, to make sure they have been understood correctly and that the business is happy the project is focused on the right goals.

The major deliverable from the strategy stage is the strategy report or strategic business requirements document but there are a number of other deliverables that could be relevant:

Draft Business Requirements
During the early part of the stage, particularly if more than one person is doing the information gathering, it may be appropriate to produce one or more drafts of the identified requirements. This will give people the chance to review and correct them.

Feedback Sessions
It is a good idea to hold presentations and feedback sessions, to tell people about the project and the preliminary findings (and get their feedback).

Strategy Report
Once all the business requirements are finalized, they need to be documented in a report that will be used as the basis for agreement with the business. This is the key deliverable from the stage.

Presentation
The findings of the stage will normally be presented to senior management in some way. This presentation will also be a deliverable in its own right.

Other Deliverables

In addition to these deliverables, there will also be the standard deliverables that are applicable to all stages. These include the End Stage Report, Next Stage Plan and the Revised Project Plan.

Stage Tasks

The tasks required in the Strategy Stage will be dependent on the deliverables that are going to be produced. The following are some typical tasks that may be needed:

1. Carry out briefings, interviews and other information gathering with the business and document them

2. Produce draft business requirements based on the results of the information gathering by combining common requirements and identifying conflicting requirements

3. Prepare for and conduct one or more feedback sessions and presentations with the business to report back what they have told you

4. Consolidate the results of feedback sessions and complete the documentation of the business requirements

5. Evolve any other recommendations that need to be made and prepare and present the findings to senior management

6. Review the progress of the stage against the stage plan, produce the next stage plan and revise the project plan, business case and risks if necessary

7. Document any lessons learned from the stage, produce the end stage report and carry out the stage review with the project sponsor or steering group

8. Again it may be appropriate to add a dummy project administration task (based on the amount of time spent on administration during the initiation stage)

Analysis Stage

During the Analysis Stage we take the strategic business requirements (produced in the Strategy Stage) and develop what will have to be done in order to meet them. Not yet how it will be done (that will come during Design), just what has to be done at this stage.

Stage Deliverables

The key deliverable from the Analysis Stage is therefore the detailed Specification of Requirements. This will allow any supplier (internal or external) or indeed the project team to propose how they will meet them.

The other deliverables that may be produced from the stage will be things such as:

- Draft Specification of Requirements

- Standards, Constraints and Design Issues

- Business Models and Prototypes

- Implementation Strategy

- Outline Test Plan

- End Stage Report

- Next Stage Plan

- Revised Project Plan

If the Design and Build Stage is going to be outsourced there will also be some form of supplier selection process involving an Invitation to Tender, Supplier Short-list, Supplier Evaluation Reports, Selection of Supplier and Agreement of Contract.

Stage Tasks

The following are the typical tasks that will need to be completed in the Analysis Stage:

1   Review existing systems, procedures, standards, constraints and potential design issues and document them

2   Investigate and develop detailed requirements, including the development of models and prototypes if necessary

3   Develop an outline test plan or strategy for how the results of the Design & Build Stage will be tested for acceptability

4   Test and evaluate any models and prototypes that have been developed for functionality and usability

5   Develop an initial implementation strategy, defining how the new system, process or product will be brought into use once developed

6   Using the outputs from the previous tasks, assemble the draft Specification of Requirements, review with the business and finalize

7   Review the progress of the project against plan, produce the next stage plan, review the risks and business case and revise the project plan

8   Prepare the End Stage Report and carry out an End Stage Review with the project sponsor

9   Project administration: a dummy task to schedule the various bits of administration work the project manager needs to do

In addition, if the project is using external suppliers you will need to run the tender process and select the supplier.

Hot tip

Make sure you involve the end users and understand how any proposed changes will affect them.

Design & Build Stage

The Specification of Requirements (from the Analysis Stage) is now used as the basis for designing how the requirements will be met. The design, once agreed, will then be built or turned into a working product, process or system.

Design Process
During the Analysis Stage we defined what will have to be done to meet the business requirements. The design process sets out how it will be done. The actual design work will depend on what the project is for, but the following processes may be relevant:

Usability
In addition to satisfying the business requirements, any solution must be usable. It is essential to involve the end users both in the design and in testing and approving the final product.

Refining the Design
Typically, the design process will run through a cycle. First refining the requirements by discussion, then identifying potential solutions to them, then developing layouts, blueprints, prototypes or designs and finally testing them for usability.

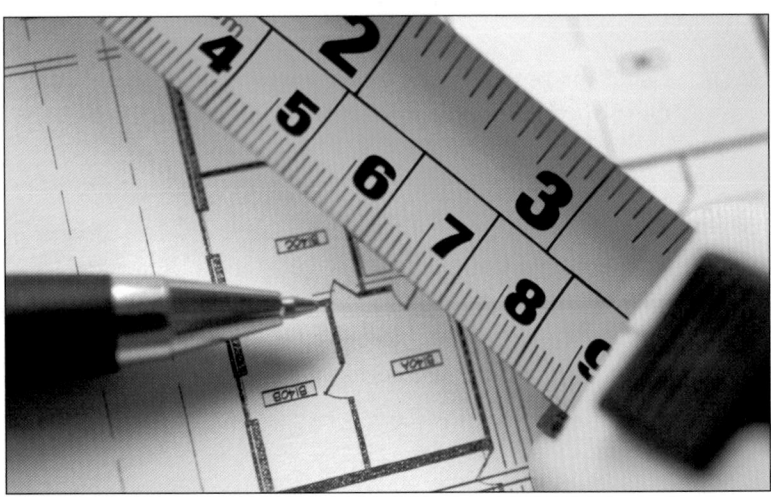

Design Deliverables
The key deliverable from the design process will be some form of Design Document, which will need to be reviewed and signed off by the business before it is built. There are a number of other deliverables that may be produced:

- Refined Requirements

- Draft Designs, Models and Prototypes

- Detailed Test Plan

- Implementation Strategy

- Training Plan

- Final Design Document

- Software, Hardware and Infrastructure Specifications

- End Stage Report

- Next Stage Plan

- Revised Project Plan

Design Tasks

The typical tasks that will need to be carried out include:

1 Refine the requirements through a process of discussion and exploration of options

2 Design how the refined requirements will be met through the build process

3 Develop layouts, plans, blueprints, scale models or prototypes to illustrate how the design could be built and review these with users

These first three tasks will tend to be reiterative, that is they will be carried out in a continuous process until all parties are satisfied or a compromise is reached. Once the design is agreed:

4 Produce the test plan, which sets out how the completed product will be verified and passed as 'fit for purpose'

5 Assemble the final Design Document and supporting material, present to the business management and end users and sign off

The Build Process

The build process is the second part of the Design & Build Stage. It takes the Business Requirements and the final Design Document, as approved by the business, and turns the design into a working product.

Build Deliverables

The main deliverables from the build process will be the final product but there will be a number of other deliverables, such as:

- Progress Reports and interim sign-off if the build process is being carried out by an external contractor

- Documentation such as user manuals, operational documentation and technical specifications

- Training Material, which may be produced by the contractor or the project team or a combination of both

- Snag Lists or fault notifications of any test failures

- Test Results documenting the acceptance and usability test completion

- Acceptance Certificate issued to an external contractor signifying the end of the build process and the start of their maintenance period

- End Stage Report

- Next Stage Plan

- Revised Project Plan

Build Tasks

The typical tasks that will be carried out during the build process include:

1 Agree the detailed designs and schedules for work with suppliers (external or internal)

2 Review progress of work with suppliers and take action to deal with any issues or exceptions

3 Receive completed work from suppliers, review and issue interim sign off for external suppliers

These first three Tasks control the allocation of work to the supplier, monitoring the supplier's progress on the work and receiving the completed work back. Concurrent with the supplier work, testing, training and documentation tasks will need to be carried out by the project team:

1 Prepare acceptance tests, perform them and review the results

2 Review and quality assure supplier's documentation

3 Produce user documentation

4 Produce and test training material and develop a detailed training plan

5 Complete the implementation strategy

6 Review progress of the project against plan, produce the next stage plan, review the risks and business case and revise the project plan

7 Prepare the End Stage Report and carry out an End Stage Review with the project sponsor or senior management (this is usually the final Go/No Go decision point)

Implementation Stage

During the Implementation Stage any necessary training is carried out and the business changes over to using the new product, system or process. The change over should leave the end users confident and ready to exploit the new product. The stage should also cover an initial period of support for the new product (typically from one to three months).

Stage Deliverables

The main deliverables from the Implementation Stage will be trained end users, completion of parallel running (if applicable) and the cut over to the new product.

The product will be formally handed over to and accepted by the business 'owner' at the end of cut-over and the project team can be officially disbanded (project closure is covered in the next chapter). Typical deliverables include:

- User Training

- Completion of Parallel Running

- Cut-over and/or Ramp up of Production

- Customer Acceptance

- End Stage Report

- Project Closure Plan

Stage Tasks

Typical tasks that will be carried out in the stage include:

1. Train the end users in the new product and give them any necessary documentation

2. Carry out any preliminary data take-on to enable the new product to function

3. Installation of production systems and any other supporting procedures

4. Prepare for and perform cut-over from the old processes to the new product

5 Support the users and operation of the new product during the critical early use period

6 Once things are running smoothly, hand over the new product to the business

7 Produce the Project Closure Plan

8 Review progress of project against plan, review and update the risks and business case and revise the project plan if necessary

9 Prepare the End Stage Report and hold the End Stage Review with the project sponsor

Planning for the implementation stage should have taken place during the earlier stages, so the main effort now is to make sure the users are properly trained and that the cut over goes smoothly. Problems and issues will occur and need to be addressed by the project team.

The end users will need a lot of support during the first few weeks of any new system or process so it is a good time to walk the floor and see how they are doing.

177

Hot tip

Stay close to and support the end users as they are the key to the success of the project.

Summary

- The project life cycle begins with project start up and progresses through a number of stages to project closure

- The project road map gives a pictorial overview of the project life cycle with a brief description of the purpose of each stage

- While a project may have as few or as many stages as needed, five is a good number to start with

- We have used Initiation, Strategy, Analysis, Design & Build and Implementation as the stage names through the book but they can be anything you or your organization likes

- The early stages of a project are crucial in establishing whether a project should go ahead or not and tend to be less costly than the later stages

- All projects should start with a short initiation stage to plan the project, confirm the business case and develop the project initiation document

- The project initiation document (PID) details what the project objectives are, how they will be achieved and how the project will be controlled

- The Strategy Stage develops the business requirements, documents them and agrees they are what the business needs

- The Analysis Stage takes the business requirements and develops them into what will have to be done to achieve them (but not yet how it will be done)

- The first part of the Design & Build Stage works out how the business requirements can be met and agrees this with the business. This may involve many iterations of the refine/design/develop cycle of tasks

- The build process then creates the business processes, product, system or whatever the project requires and gains the business and user acceptance to the finished product

- The Implementation Stage then implements the new product, training the users, replacing any old methods with the new and supporting the new process while it settles down

11 Project Closure

This final, short chapter deals with closing a project down in an orderly fashion.

Closing the Project

And so at last the end is near and we can see the final curtain. There just remains the matter of winding up the project in a controlled way.

Standard Change Curve

There will usually be a big effort required by the project team in the early part of implementation. But both the team and the end users should also be very positive about the change (as long as they have been fully involved). But beware, for this is just the first stage in the change process. This is illustrated in the following diagram:

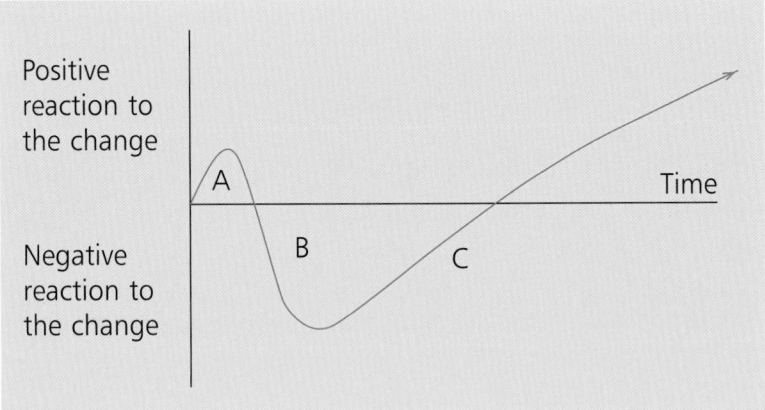

The diagram illustrates the way most people react to change, when they have been fully involved or consulted on it. It shows the three stages of Optimism (A), Pessimism (B) and Realism (C).

Optimism

As long as the people concerned have been involved and do not feel threatened by the change, there is an initial period of optimism (marked A on the diagram). Here everyone concerned with the project has high expectations and will be excited about the new product.

This period of time is usually very brief as quite soon hard realities and problems start to crop up and teething problems begin to occur. There is also an additional work effort in getting used to a new way of doing things. This starts to reduce the level of optimism, which seems to erode day by day and then begins to turn into pessimism as they start to expect the worst.

Pessimism

As people move into the period of pessimism (marked B on the diagram) they begin to think it might all be a big mistake. They start to question the new way and say how much better, and maybe easier, the old way was. This is where the project team really does have to work hard at encouraging people and resolving any problems and issues quickly so that they can move on to the third period.

Realism

Once the issues are addressed and problems start to get resolved, confidence will begin to grow again as the end users get used to the new way of working and begin to see the benefits. This is referred to as the period of realism (marked C on the diagram) and gradually they begin to like the new way and become positive again.

Project Closure

Once the people operating the new product have reached this stage it is time to close the project. If not, there is the danger that it will just keep on rolling along and never get finished. There will always be little enhancements that can be made and little issues that need fixing. The devil really does make work for idle hands!

Documentation

There is another, equally important, reason for project closure and that is to make sure that everything that needs to be done has been done and documented. This is essential to allow the project team to move on and the business to take full ownership of the new product.

Lessons Learned

It is also the ideal time to capture any lessons learned from the project while they are still fresh in people's minds. They need to be captured, recognized and acted on by the organization, so that future projects can benefit from them.

Formal Project Closure

The reason for a formal project closure is that the project and the project team then cease to exist. Everything returns to 'business as usual' and the project team can go back to (or be reassigned to) other duties within the organization. It also means that all the loose ends have been tidied up.

Hot tip

It really is worth while the project manager and team members 'walking the floor' during this period.

Hot tip

Make sure you have agreed in advance who will be taking ownership of the new product.

Project Closure

We identified the main reasons for closing a project in the previous topic. In this topic we will explore the project closure process in a bit more detail and identify the deliverables and tasks involved.

Project Deliverables

All major and minor deliverables from the project should have been identified and their production tracked. Formal confirmation that they have been produced to the required quality, and have been accepted by the business, should be documented. It is not unusual to find that some project deliverables have been 'left in limbo'. Checking and confirming all deliverables will ensure they have all been completed and signed-off.

Support Arrangements

The required support arrangements for the business should have been identified as part of their requirements. These support and maintenance arrangements should now have been set up to operate for the life of the product. The arrangements should operate fully within the business and not require any form of ongoing support from members of the project team (unless the person concerned is moving into a new role to provide it).

Lessons Learned

There will normally be a lot of lessons learned during the course of a project. From the business point of view, it is essential that these lessons are not lost. While the project manager might well remember and benefit from them in future, it is also important that the whole business does too. Therefore, any lessons learned during the project (however painful) should be recorded, consolidated and passed on to the appropriate person or group within the business for onward communication. This forms a good basis for an organization's developing maturity in project management. It marks the difference between a good organization and an indifferent one.

Benefit Assessment

The benefits should start to occur once the new product has settled in, so benefits measurement should begin following implementation. If this is not done then there can be no real assessment of the business benefits of the project. It is usual for any new system, product or way of working to take some time

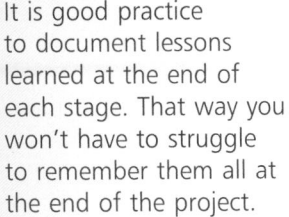

Don't forget

It is good practice to document lessons learned at the end of each stage. That way you won't have to struggle to remember them all at the end of the project.

before the full benefits are achieved so a date, at some specific time in the future, should be agreed when this will take place.

Close the Cost Center

It means no further project expenditure, or other form of resource usage, can take place. Any budget authorizations or cost centers set up for the project should be closed (or frozen) so that the final cost of the project can be determined.

Early Project Closure

If, for whatever reason, the project is terminated before completion, it should still be formally closed. In addition, the reasons for the early closure should be documented together with the agreed way of dealing with the situation.

Closure Deliverables

So that is what is involved in closing a project. The following are the deliverables that should be produced:

- Business Acceptance of the new product or process

- End Project Report with lessons learned and follow-on action recommendations

Closure Tasks

The typical tasks that will need to be carried out include:

1 Completion, sign-off and archiving of all project documents and files

2 Obtain business acceptance for the product and hand over to operation and support groups

3 Update the project plan with the final actual results of the project

4 Produce the end project report with lessons learned and any follow-on action recommendations and schedule and hold the end project review with the sponsor

5 Plan, schedule and agree the post-project review with the project sponsor and business

Hot tip

Schedule a final 'thank you' celebration for the project team and invite the project sponsor.

and finally

In this book we have tried to deal with all the relevant topics that apply to project management. Some of these are quite serious but project management can also be fun, so in that light:

20 Laws of Project Management

While the following are slightly 'tongue-in-cheek' there is an element of truth in each of them and they will help to reinforce the topics in this book:

1 Fast, cheap, good: pick any two!

2 The project would not have been started if the business had been told the truth about the cost and time scale

3 A two-year project will take three years; a three-year project will never finish

4 Never underestimate the ability of senior management to buy a bad idea and fail to buy a good idea

5 A badly planned project will take three times as long as planned. A well planned one will only take twice as long

6 If it weren't for the 'last minute', nothing would ever get done

7 It takes one woman nine months to have a baby. It cannot be done in one month by putting nine women on the project

8 The same work under the same conditions will be estimated differently by ten different project managers or by one project manager at ten different times

9 Nothing is impossible for the person who doesn't have to do it

10 The more desperate the situation the more optimistic the situatee

Beware

Throwing more people at a late project will make it later still.

Beware

Avoid optimism, things do not magically get better.

11 If it looks like a duck, walks like a duck and quacks like a duck, it probably is a duck

12 A change freeze is like the abominable snowman: it is a myth and melts when heat is applied

13 An end user will tell you anything you ask about, but nothing more

Hot tip

Keep on asking questions until you are sure there is nothing more they can tell you.

14 Of several possible interpretations of a communication, the least convenient is always the correct one

15 What you don't know does hurt you

16 The conditions attached to a promise are forgotten, only the promise is remembered

17 There's never enough time to do it right first time but there's always enough time to go back and do it again

18 I know that you believe that you understand what you think I said but I am not sure you realize that what you heard is not what I meant

19 What is not on paper has not been said

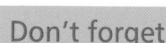

Don't forget

If it's important, back it up in writing.

20 There are no good project managers, only lucky ones

Hot tip

In the light of Law 20: be lucky!

Summary

- Remember the standard change curve and that the project team and the end users are likely to go through this after the new product or process goes live

- Be careful not to mistake the initial period of optimism for confidence in the new product, there will be teething problems and the new process will take longer at first

- As the teething problems start to occur and the end users hit problems and issues with the new process, make sure you are there 'walking the floor' to pick up the issues and help them

- As realism sets in and people get used to the 'new way', encourage them to see the benefits and recognize that their effort was all worthwhile

- Once the new process is running smoothly close the project down or it will roll on forever!

- Make sure everything has been documented and all the deliverables have been completed and accepted

- Set up the support arrangements for the new process in advance so that the people who will be responsible for it are ready to go

- Obtain the business sign-off for the project showing that they have accepted it and it can be closed

- Review the lessons learned for the whole project as well as for the process of bringing the new product into production use and document them for the benefit of the organization

- Set up a plan for reviewing the achievements of the expected benefits some time after the project has been completed and agree this with the project sponsor

- Close the cost center so people can't continue to charge things to the project and you have the final cost

- Produce the end project report documenting the final results and costs of the project against the budget

- Take the project team out for a celebration meal to thank them and include the project sponsor

Hot tip

With luck the sponsor will pick up the tab.

Index

187

H

I

J

K

L

M

N

O

U

V

W